Policy Papers
in International Affairs

NUMBER 19

THE

Atlantic Alliance, Nuclear Weapons & European Attitudes

REEXAMINING THE
CONVENTIONAL WISDOM

Wallace J. Thies

Institute of
International Studies
UNIVERSITY OF CALIFORNIA • BERKELEY

In sponsoring the Policy Papers in International Affairs series, the Institute of International Studies reasserts its commitment to a vigorous policy debate by providing a forum for innovative approaches to important policy issues. The views expressed in each paper are those of the author only, and publication in this series does not constitute endorsement by the Institute.

International Standard Book Number 0-87725-519-9

Library of Congress Catalog Card Number 83-82915

CONTENTS

Acknowledgments

An earlier version of this paper was presented at the meeting of the Northern California Political Science Association at Hayward State University, May 7, 1983. Ernst Haas, Kenneth Waltz, Paul Seabury, and Gregory Luebbert read the earlier version and offered many helpful comments and suggestions. Responsibility for the final product is, of course, mine alone.

W. J. T.

INTRODUCTION

It has become part of the conventional wisdom concerning the North Atlantic Alliance that the condition of the Alliance as it entered the 1980s was worse than at any time in its history. Of all the sources of strain within the Alliance, the one that has engendered the most controversy in Europe and the most commentary by observers of the Alliance's affairs was the December 1979 decision by the North Atlantic Council to deploy 108 Pershing II ballistic missiles in West Germany and 464 ground-launched cruise missiles in West Germany, Italy, Great Britain, Belgium, and the Netherlands. Mass demonstrations in Europe in reaction to that decision, expressions of anti-NATO and anti-American sentiments by some of the demonstrators, and an apparent rise in neutralist and pacifist sentiment in Western Europe convinced many observers that the Alliance was facing one of its most dangerous tests.[1] Some even suggested that the Alliance had already virtually ceased to exist, and that it was only a matter of time before the funeral rites were held.[2]

And yet it has also become part of the conventional wisdom concerning NATO that nuclear weapons issues have always strained the Alliance — both in terms of relations among member states and in terms of relations between the governments of member states and their electorates.[3] In the first category would be the controversy over the American request to station Thor and Jupiter intermediate-range ballistic missiles (IRBMs) in Europe in the late-1950s, the proposal for a fleet of missile-firing surface ships (the Multilateral Force), and the Kennedy administration's efforts to deemphasize nuclear weapons in favor of a strategy that placed greater reliance on conventional forces. In the second category would be the controversy that followed the Alliance's December 1954 decision to place greater reliance on nuclear weapons for defense against a Soviet attack, the

1

mass demonstrations and protests in West Germany in 1958 which followed the Adenauer government's decision to request that the Bundeswehr be equipped with tactical nuclear weapons, and the Aldermaston marches in Great Britain. The protests and mass demonstrations of 1981 and 1982 may have seemed to be an unprecedented strain on the Alliance only because they followed a period of nearly two decades—from the early 1960s to the end of the 1970s—when nuclear concerns were muted by the rise of detente in Europe and European publics were generally quiescent.

This suggests the two questions which will be the focus of this paper. First, is the current controversy over modernizing the Alliance's long-range theater nuclear forces (LRTNF) in Europe so much more serious than previous disputes that it warrants the conclusion that the condition of the Alliance is worse now than ever before? Second, is it possible to draw from the record of previous Alliance crises any suggestions or lessons that are relevant to managing or resolving the current controversy over the role of nuclear weapons in the Alliance's strategy for deterrence and defense in Europe?

I

THE ATLANTIC ALLIANCE AND LRTNF:
IS THIS CRISIS REALLY DIFFERENT?

At first glance, the controversy engendered by the Alliance's decision to deploy new continental-range nuclear missiles in Europe appears to be a tangled skein of conflicting views and mutual recriminations, in which the divergent concerns of the United States and its European allies have interacted in such a way as to heighten tensions within the Alliance. The LRTNF issue was first raised in public, albeit indirectly, by Chancellor Helmut Schmidt of West Germany in a lecture delivered in London in October 1977.[4] The European members of the Alliance were at the time concerned both with the overall foreign policy of the Carter administration and especially with the possibility that the SALT II negotiations would leave the Soviet SS-20 IRBM and Backfire bomber unconstrained, while placing limits on the range and deployment by the Alliance of ground- and sea-launched cruise missiles, which the Europeans saw as obvious counters to the new Soviet systems. American officials were at first unconvinced of the need for new continental-range nuclear missiles in Europe, but eventually the Carter administration became committed to the program as a way of asserting American leadership within the Alliance and demonstrating that the Alliance could still act in concert after the fiasco over the neutron bomb.[5]

Discussions on the number and types of forces that would be required to offset Soviet SS-20 and Backfire deployments were conducted during 1978 and 1979 by the Alliance's High-Level Group (HLG); a second, parallel group—the Special Group—was created in April 1979 to consider possible arms limitation agreements on

3

LRTNF deployments.[6] By the summer of 1979, the participants in the discussions within the HLG had reached agreement on the goals and characteristics of the LRTNF program, thus laying the groundwork for the formal decision at the December 1979 meeting of the North Atlantic Council to deploy in Europe a mixed force of 572 Pershing II ballistic missiles and ground-launched cruise missiles while simultaneously offering to engage in arms control negotiations with the Soviets to limit LRTNF deployments. Despite efforts by the Carter administration to produce a resounding Alliance consensus in support of the LRTNF program, the planned deployments came to be seen by many in Europe as an American strategic initiative that would allow the United States, which was to be the sole owner and operator of the missiles, to launch a nuclear strike on the Soviet Union from bases in Europe, thus preserving American territory as a sanctuary from Soviet nuclear retaliation. These sentiments were heightened by the collapse of Soviet-American detente in 1980 and the apparent fixation of the Carter administration on events in Southwest Asia (especially the presence of Soviet troops in Afghanistan), which raised fears in Europe of a Soviet-American clash that could start outside Europe but would engulf Europe also.

These fears were at the heart of the protests and demonstrations in Europe in 1981 and 1982 in opposition to the planned missile deployments. Reagan administration officials responded by inveighing against the spread of neutralist and pacifist sentiment in Europe and by complaining that the European members of the Alliance no longer seemed to care about their own defense. These complaints, along with some careless remarks about the possibility of a limited nuclear war in Europe and the Administration's seeming lack of interest in arms control, provided supporting evidence for those in Europe who argued that the United States had become bellicose, militarist, inclined toward nuclear war-fighting, and an untrustworthy partner. As neutralist and pacifist sentiment in Western Europe seemingly increased, Congressional and Administration officials in the United States responded with warnings of a possible withdrawal of American troops stationed there.

There can be no question that the Alliance has been sorely troubled of late. But do the protests and demonstrations against the deployment of new nuclear missiles in Europe, the expressions of anti-NATO and anti-American sentiments by the protesters, and the apparent spread of neutralist and pacifist sentiment in Western Europe constitute unprecedented strains on the Alliance, or are they merely the latest manifestations of tensions that have always troubled the Alliance? Is the condition of the Alliance really worse now than ever before, or are its recent troubles simply the latest in a long series of crises, all of which until now have been surmounted and most of which have quickly been forgotten as new crises have emerged?

THE GROWTH OF NEUTRALIST/PACIFIST SENTIMENT IN WESTERN EUROPE

Almost from the time the North Atlantic Alliance was founded, observers have been discovering ominous trends, problems that are growing increasingly acute, and contradictions that are sharpening with each passing year. These claims are only rarely accompanied by the kind of evidence that would permit a disinterested observer to verify whether changes in the condition of the Alliance are actually occurring in the predicted direction. Instead, these types of judgments about the Alliance are often based on evidence that is largely impressionistic, such as a sampling of media commentary in a member country, or interviews with government officials and non-governmental elites who are sufficiently dissatisfied with the Alliance's performance to air their complaints to a sympathetic listener. Sometimes the results of a recent opinion survey are cited, as if a shift in the climate of opinion could be deduced from a single sampling.[7]

A good example of the failure to provide the kind of evidence needed to support conclusions about the condition of the Alliance can be found in recent claims that neutralist and pacifist sentiments have become widespread in Western Europe as a consequence of the Alliance's December 1979 decision to deploy new continental-range nuclear missiles in Europe. Elite and mass attitudes in Western Europe are often described as if they have shifted radically in recent years

5

toward growing sympathy for neutralism and pacifism and increased hostility to the Alliance and what it represents. Sometimes these shifts in attitudes are said to reflect a secular trend; sometimes they are described in terms of generational change; sometimes both explanations are used by the same author.[8] Two consequences are usually deduced from the changes which are said to be occurring in the political climate in Western Europe. First, the governments of the European members of NATO are said to be increasingly reluctant to take the steps required to preserve a military balance in Europe, such as increasing defense spending and providing bases for the new nuclear missiles whose deployment was agreed upon in December 1979. Second, following from the first, the military balance in Europe is said to be tilting steadily in favor of the Soviet Union, a process which, if allowed to continue, will either relegate NATO to irrelevance or result in the breakup of the Alliance as the European members seek an accommodation with the Soviet Union.

One difficulty with claims that the climate of opinion in Western Europe has been changing recently in the direction of greater sympathy for neutralism/pacifism is that they are almost never accompanied by the kind of data that would permit systematic comparisons to determine if the change that is allegedly taking place is really occurring. This is a crucial omission, because even a cursory review of the history of the Alliance suggests that neutralist and pacifist sentiments have always been attractive to a sizable segment of the publics of Western Europe. Edmond Taylor's reference to the "stealthy spread of European neutralism that seriously disturbs some NATO authorities" could easily be taken as a description of the situation in Western Europe in 1981 or 1982, except that it was written in 1955, shortly after the North Atlantic Council's December 1954 decision to allow Allied military officers to base their planning on the early use of nuclear weapons by the Alliance in the event of a Soviet attack.[9]

Moreover, neutralist and pacifist sentiments are difficult to measure accurately since the wording of questions used in public opinion surveys may offer subtle cues to the respondent as to the "correct" or "appropriate" response. Depending on the polls used and the time periods surveyed, it is possible to make a strong argument that neutralist and pacifist sentiments have actually been declining rather than increasing in strength in Western Europe.

Is There a Trend Toward Neutralism in Western Europe? The apparent growth in neutralist sentiment in Western Europe in recent years has been paralleled by a proliferation of catchwords and phrases intended to dramatize the changes supposedly occurring: "Euro-neutralism," "Hollanditis," "Denmarkization," "Finland-ization." As these labels suggest, the changes supposedly occurring in Western Europe are often described in no uncertain terms, as if there were no room for doubt that a shift toward neutralism is taking place.

Public opinion surveys in Western Europe in recent years have presented a much different picture, however. The results of opinion surveys have often seemed to contradict each other, making it difficult to discern what Europeans are thinking about the Alliance and what changes, if any, have been taking place. Some surveys have suggested that the level of support for the Alliance remains unchanged, such as a May 1981 survey in which 80 percent of West German respondents expressed a preference for remaining in the Alliance, while only 6 percent opted for withdrawal—exactly the same result as in a January 1969 survey.[10] Other surveys have suggested a dramatic erosion in support for the Alliance, such as a January 1983 survey in which majorities in West Germany and the Netherlands and pluralities in Britain and France (and a near-plurality in the United States) said they would favor a move toward neutralism in Western Europe (see Table 1).[11]

The key to reconciling these divergent outcomes lies in the multiple meanings that can be associated with "neutralism." Neutralism is a difficult concept to define, and the wording of questions used in public opinion surveys can have a significant effect on the responses. For example, large segments of the publics of Western Europe have traditionally favored keeping their countries out of quarrels between the United States and the Soviet Union. In the early 1950s, one-third of West German respondents on average took the position that Germany should stay out of the East-West struggle; the percentage of West German respondents preferring neutrality in the event of an East-West war rose from 37 in September 1952 to

Table 1

*Some have said that Western Europe would be safer if it moved toward neu-
tralism in the East-West conflict. Others argue that such a move would be
dangerous. Would you, yourself, favor or oppose a move toward neutralism in
Western Europe?*

	Percent Response	
Country	Favor	Oppose
West Germany	57%	43%
Netherlands	53	32
Great Britain	45	42
France	43	41
United States	41	44

Source: Surveys by the Gallup Organization for *Newsweek* magazine, 1/31/83.

46 in early 1954 to 53 in October 1954.[12] In a February 1964
survey, 42 percent of West German respondents thought neutrality
between East and West was preferable to friendship with the United
States, while 49 percent preferred friendship with the United
States.[13] In an April 1980 survey, majorities in Britain and France
and a plurality in West Germany preferred that their governments do
everything possible to stay out of quarrels between the United States
and the Soviet Union.[14] And in a December 1980 survey, 63 percent
of French respondents said they would have their government ask
the Soviet Union to permit France to stay out of an American-Soviet
conflict rather than side with the United States.[15]

However, when asked whether NATO was "still essential" for
the security of their country, majorities in Belgium, Denmark, Britain,
West Germany, Italy, and the Netherlands and a plurality in France
responded that it was essential in surveys conducted in 1980 and
1981 (see Table 2).[16] When confronted with an explicit choice
between remaining in NATO and being neutral, majorities in Britain,
West Germany, Italy, and the Netherlands preferred NATO over
neutrality in a March 1981 survey (see Table 3).[17] Only in France

Table 2

Date/Country	Percent Response	
	NATO still essential for security	NATO not essential for security
October 1980		
Belgium	57%	19%
Denmark	70	19
France	44	34
March 1981		
Britain	70	15
West Germany	62	20
Italy	59	38
Norway	66	21
Netherlands	62	15

Source: U.S. International Communications Agency (Danish survey conducted by Danish Gallup Institute).

Table 3

All things considered, do you think it is better for our country to belong to NATO, the Western defense alliance, or would it be better for us to get out of NATO and become a neutral country?

Country	Date/Percent Response			
	March 1981		July 1981	
	Stay in NATO	Be Neutral	Stay in NATO	Be Neutral
West Germany	67%	14%	64%	18%
Great Britain	67	20	59	29
Netherlands	62	17	56	25
Italy	60	31	49	42
France	45	40	33	51

Source: U.S. International Communications Agency.

was opinion evenly divided on this issue. The percentage preferring to remain in NATO declined in all five countries between March and July 1981, but one should be careful not to read too much into short-term fluctuations in support for the alliance.

For one thing, the results of opinion surveys can vary substantially depending on the date of the survey and/or the wording of the question. As Table 4 indicates, the level of support among Dutch respondents for remaining in NATO held steady at 76 percent between July 1974 and December 1980.[18] Between December 1980 and October 1981, the percentage of Dutch respondents preferring that the Netherlands remain in NATO declined from 76 to 69, but by January 1982 the percentage favoring continued NATO membership had returned to 76.

Table 4

Holland is a member of NATO, the North Atlantic Treaty Organization. What do you think: Should our country remain a member of NATO or leave it?

| | Date/Percent | | | | | |
Response	July 1974	October 1979	January 1980	December 1980	October 1981	January 1982
Remain in NATO	76%	76%	76%	76%	69%	76%
Leave NATO	9	12	14	12	12	13
No opinion	15	12	10	12	19	11

Source: Netherlands Institute of Public Opinion.

Second, in those cases where trend data are available, they suggest that a preference for the Alliance over neutrality may have increased over time. In Italy, respondents in an October 1958 poll favored the Alliance over neutrality by a margin of 50 to 25 percent, compared to 60 to 31 percent in March 1981.[19] In West Germany, as the data in Table 5 suggest, opinion was evenly divided between maintaining a military alliance with the United States and neutrality until 1973; since 1974 roughly one-half of the respondents in surveys of adult West Germans have favored maintaining the alliance with the United States while only about one-third have favored neutrality.[20] When asked to choose between good relations with America and good relations with Russia, the percentage of West Germans believing the former more important than the latter increased from 52 in 1975 to 63 in 1979 to 65 in 1981.[21]

Table 5

Which do you think would be the better foreign policy: Should [West Germany] remain militarily allied with the United States or should we attempt to be neutral?

Response	Year/Percent							
	1961	1965	1969	1973	1974	1975	1978	1981
Military alliance	40%	46%	44%	41%	51%	49%	57%	55%
Be neutral	42	37	38	42	38	36	27	31
Undecided	18	17	18	17	11	15	16	14

Source: Allensbach Institute for Demoscopy.

The reporting of poll data in scholarly journals and opinion summaries can lag behind the survey date by up to a year, and it may be that the trend toward neutralism in Western Europe has only recently begun to gather momentum. The results of readily available opinion polls, however, suggest that there has not as yet been a dramatic shift toward neutralism on the part of European publics.

Generational Change in Western Europe. It could be argued that neutralist sentiment in Western Europe is particularly widespread among younger members of the public—namely, the "successor generation" that came to political maturity in the 1970s and early 1980s. Since respondents under 30 would constitute only a small fraction of a national sample of adults in a West European state, public opinion surveys may provide a misleading picture of the political climate in

Western Europe. In particular, national surveys of adult opinion may not accurately tap the changes currently taking place as the postwar generation is gradually replaced by a new generation whose views were shaped by a vastly different set of experiences.

The "successor generation" argument starts from the premise that the generation that came to political maturity in the 1940s was strongly influenced by memories of war and occupation.[22] In the countries that had been overrun by Germany, the lesson was that defense and military preparedness were essential to prevent a repetition of the tragedy of 1940; hence the strong support for NATO as a military alliance in the Netherlands, Belgium, Norway, Denmark, and so on during the 1950s and 1960s. In both the former occupied countries and in Germany itself, the United States was seen as savior, protector, and a model to be followed in the reconstruction of their societies.

The Vietnam war, according to this argument, was the turning point that led to a sharp revision in the attitudes of younger Europeans toward the United States. Instead of being seen as savior and protector, the United States was now seen as the oppressor of Third World peoples striving for liberation. Moreover, the generation that came of age in the 1970s had no memories of war and occupation; instead, their views were shaped by the years of detente in Europe, when the Soviet Union came to be seen not as a military threat but as a predictable, if not especially attractive, neighbor. Hence, the "successor generation" sees little need for defense and military preparedness; it has instead become enamored with unilateral disarmament and the notion that Europe should set an example for the superpowers of how to live in peace, unencumbered by armaments and the quarrels of the past.

Available poll data suggest that neutralist sentiment is more widespread among younger West Europeans than among the older generation. Thus a March 1981 survey found a direct relationship between the age of the respondent and preference for continued NATO membership among university-educated respondents in Britain, France, West Germany, Italy, the Netherlands, and Norway (see Table 6).[23] Respondents over age 50 in all six countries overwhelmingly rejected neutrality in favor of NATO membership; respondents in the middle-age grouping (35-49) were somewhat more inclined to pick neutrality over NATO; and those in the 18-34 age group were the most likely to prefer neutrality. But even in the 18-34 age group, majorities in all six countries preferred continued NATO membership to neutrality.

Table 6

All things considered, do you think it is better for our country to belong to NATO, the Western defense alliance, or would it be better for us to get out of NATO and become a neutral country?

	Age Group (University-Educated Respondents)/Percent					
	18-34		35-49		50 & Older	
Country	NATO	Neutral	NATO	Neutral	NATO	Neutral
United Kingdom	62%	27%	70%	21%	86%	5%
France	53	33	61	34	79	18
West Germany	59	28	63	25	95	5
Italy	56	39	82	18	81	14
Netherlands	64	30	65	21	86	5
Norway	59	36	75	16	88	7

Source: U.S. International Communications Agency, March 1981

Moreover, in a fall 1980 survey, only 2 percent of West German youth (up to age 24) expressed a preference for leaving NATO, as opposed to 11 percent who preferred a "more solid" NATO and 74 percent who preferred an unchanged NATO (see Table 7).[24] Only 6 percent of West German youth considered the presence of American troops in Europe "unimportant" or "harmful," compared with 72 percent who felt their presence "indispensable" or "important." In a 1979 survey, younger West Germans expressed markedly more pro-American views than did older people: 57 percent of the 16-29 age-group said they liked Americans as opposed to only 42 percent of those 60 and over.[25] Where the younger generation in West Germany differs from their parents is not in their dislike for the United States

Table 7

Should [West Germany] belong to an unchanged NATO, or should we try to gain a more loosened or a more solid NATO, or do you think we should leave NATO?

	Percent	
Response	Total	Youth (Under 24)
Unchanged NATO	81%	74%
More solid NATO	10	11
More loosened NATO	4	7
Leave NATO	1	2

What are your views on the role of American troops in Europe?

	Percent	
Response	Total	Youth (Under 24)
Indispensable	33%	26%
Important	48	46
Of minor importance	11	18
Unimportant	3	4
Harmful	2	2

Source: Werner Kaltefleiter, "German Divisions," *Policy Review*, Fall 1981.

but in their unwillingness to submit to American wishes. As Table 8 indicates, 43 percent of the 16-29 age-group in a 1981 survey agreed that "it is no longer compatible with the new role of Germany that we submit ourselves in all areas to the American leadership," as compared to only 26 percent of those 60 and over.[26]

The "successor generation" argument may thus be wrong on two counts: (1) in its claim that anti-NATO sentiments are widespread among the younger generation and (2) in its suggestion that the older generation was eager to embrace American values, institu-

Table 8

Two people are discussing the relationship between the United States and [West Germany]. Which of the two statements reflects your thoughts more accurately?

	Age Group/Percent Response				
Choices	Total	16-29	30-44	45-59	60 & Up
We must continue to lend firm support to the United States.	48%	38%	50%	56%	49%
It is no longer compatible with the new role of Germany that we submit ourselves in all areas to the American leadership	35	43	38	33	26
Undecided	17	19	12	11	25

Source: Allensbach Institute for Demoscopy.

tions, and policies. In West Germany at least, the older generation supported entry into NATO as the path to the restoration of German sovereignty and self-respect, but this did not necessarily indicate affection for the country that had bombed Germany's cities and occupied it after the war. The younger generation, while more skeptical about the need for the Alliance and less willing to be subservient to American policy, tends to look more favorably on the United States, which they remember only as an ally rather than as a conqueror.

European Passivism. The corollary of the claim that neutralist sentiment has become increasingly widespread in Western Europe in recent years is the argument that the governments of the European members of the Alliance have become increasingly unwilling to take the politically distasteful steps necessary to maintain a military balance in Europe, and that the Alliance is thus inexorably slipping into a position of inferiority vis-à-vis the Warsaw Pact. Warnings of actual

15

or prospective Soviet military superiority have been an almost constant feature of policymaking within the Alliance since the signing of the North Atlantic Treaty in 1949, but recently these warnings have taken increasingly dramatic form. The "Dutch disease," defined as an aversion to spending money on defense, is said to be spreading throughout Western Europe—to Denmark, Norway, West Germany, and France. Others speak more ominously of the actual or impending "Finlandization" of Western Europe.[27]

Claims of this kind misrepresent the situation in Europe; they are also misleading in their efforts to apportion blame between the United States and its allies for the Alliance's supposed inability to maintain a military balance with the Warsaw Pact. They oversimplify in three ways: (1) by neglecting to take account of the strategy the Alliance has relied on for deterrence and defense in Central Europe; (2) by failing to supply needed historical perspective; and (3) by treating sensationalist leaks to the press as if they were complete and accurate representations of the Alliance's policies.[28] Both the United States and its European allies have adjusted the level of their military efforts upward and downward in response to changes in the level of international tensions, changes in military technology, and developments in other parts of the world. While there have always been disagreements among members of the Alliance as to the level of effort required to balance Soviet military power and how that effort should be distributed among NATO members, a review of the Alliance's efforts to maintain a military balance in Europe does not suggest that it has recently lost the ability to take the steps necessary to maintain such a balance. And while Soviet power has increased relative to that of the United States and its allies, that outcome does not appear to have been exclusively or even largely the fault of the European members of the Alliance.

The Alliance has never sought to match the Warsaw Pact man-for-man and tank-for-tank along the Central Front in Europe. Instead, NATO strategy ever since the early 1950s has been to maintain sufficient active-duty forces along the Central Front to require the Soviets to bring up sizable reinforcements prior to launching an attack. Movement of such forces would require several weeks and would almost certainly be noticed by the NATO countries, which would enable them to mobilize their own reserves as well as bring over reinforcements from North America.

Under the stimulus of the Korean War, the combined armed forces of the NATO countries increased from about 4.2 million in 1950 to 6.7 million in 1953. By comparison, the combined armed forces of the Soviet Union and its East European allies were estimated to be about 6.0 million in 1954.[29] No single measure can capture the complexities involved in assessing the relative military capabilities of NATO and the Warsaw Pact, but a comparison of total regular armed forces is revealing of the overall level of effort being made by each side and of the forces that could be brought to bear relatively quickly in the event of a conflict.

The armed forces of the NATO countries declined in size after 1953, but this was the result of policy decisions rather than an iron law of demography. On the assumption that the next war would inevitably be nuclear, and that nuclear weapons could substitute for manpower, the Eisenhower administration sharply reduced the size of American forces. Total American active-duty forces fell from roughly 3.5 million in 1953 to 2.5 million in 1960. Most of the cuts were made in the ground forces: the Army declined from 1.5 million in 1953 to 870,000 in 1960, while the Marines fell from 243,000 in 1954 to 175,000 in 1960. British forces peaked at about 900,000 in 1953, declining to about 520,000 in 1960.[30]

Despite these reductions, the conventional balance in Europe did not tilt in favor of the Warsaw Pact. Soviet forces were also cut back in the years following Stalin's death, as were the forces of the East European states. Soviet forces peaked at about 5.0 million in 1955, declining to about 3.6 million in 1960. Polish forces declined from about 500,000 in 1950 to about 200,000 in 1960, while the Hungarian army of about 200,000 was "virtually disbanded" as a result of the popular uprising there in 1956.[31] As of Eisenhower's last year in office (1960), the combined armed forces of the NATO countries were roughly one-third again as large as those of the Warsaw Pact (see Appendix, pp. 47-51 below). Along the Central Front, German rearmament resulted in an increase in the number of active-duty NATO divisions from 15 in 1953 to 22 by 1960 and 27 by 1964, backed by an infrastructure of airfields, pipelines, and communications links, plus supporting units and reservist divisions. The 22 or so Soviet divisions in East Germany could not have overwhelmed the NATO forces deployed along the Central Front without large-scale reinforcements, which would have required several weeks to move forward and would have constituted strategic warning that would have allowed the NATO countries to bring up reinforcements from their own larger pool of active-duty and reserve forces.[32]

The long-term viability of the Alliance's strategy for deterrence and defense in Europe was threatened by a series of events set in motion during the mid-1960s as a result of the emergence of detente in Europe and American involvement in the war in Vietnam. Between 1964 and 1968, Belgium, Britain, Canada, and France all reduced the size of their ground forces on the continent; these reductions were only partly offset by increases in West German and Dutch forces. The United States also substantially reduced its forces in Western Europe in order to meet the demands of the war in Southeast Asia. The U.S. Seventh Army in West Germany was reduced from 240,000 in 1963 to 210,000 in 1968, and U.S. tactical airpower in Europe was cut from about 1,000 aircraft in 1966 to about 450 in 1969. Overall, the number of American military personnel in Europe declined from 436,000 in 1964 to 314,000 in 1968.[33]

In the short run, these reductions do not appear to have adversely affected the military balance in Europe. During the 1960s the NATO countries routinely maintained combined armed forces one-third to one-half again as large as those of the Warsaw Pact (see Appendix). Even if U.S. increases for the Vietnam War were excluded, the NATO countries still maintained roughly 30 percent more men under arms than the Warsaw Pact. In the Center Region, NATO in 1968 had slightly more men under arms in combat and support units than did the Warsaw Pact, and the Warsaw Pact's advantage in tanks was offset by NATO advantages in numbers of armored personnel carriers, artillery, and vehicles, as well as by a significant NATO qualitative advantage in tactical airpower.[34]

Between 1968 and 1977, the combined armed forces of the

Warsaw Pact countries increased from 4,273,000 to 4,751,000 (see Appendix). More troubling for the Alliance was the increase in the offensive striking power of Soviet ground and tactical air forces. Even though the combined armed forces of the NATO countries were larger than those of the Warsaw Pact, the latter had achieved a numerical advantage in manpower in combat units along the Central Front, in part because of geographical asymmetries between the two alliances and in part because of structural differences in the armed forces each maintained. In 1969, for example, the combat and direct support forces available to the Warsaw Pact in the Center and Northern Regions were nearly one-third again as large as the corresponding NATO forces (see Table 9). The NATO countries, in contrast, had a sizable manpower advantage in the Southern Region.

During the 1970s the Warsaw Pact countries significantly increased the number of tanks deployed in Eastern Europe and in the European military districts of the Soviet Union. As Table 9 indicates, between 1969 and 1977, the number of troops in combat and direct support units deployed by the Warsaw Pact in the Center and Northern Regions increased by only 2 percent, while the number of tanks increased by 64 percent. While the number of Soviet tactical aircraft deployed in Eastern Europe increased by only about 15 percent between 1967 and 1977, the Soviets increased the offensive striking power of their tactical air units by replacing older, single-purpose aircraft with modern multi-role aircraft with greatly improved radius and payload.[35] The effect of these developments was to improve the ability of the Soviets to launch an attack across the Central Front that would come with little or no warning.

These increases in the size and quality of Warsaw Pact forces were not matched by the NATO countries. Instead, the combined armed forces of the NATO countries declined in size for nine consecutive years between 1968 and 1977 (see Appendix). Most of the NATO countries reduced the size of their military establishments during this period, but the reductions by the United States were proportionately larger than those by the European members of NATO, with the exception of Portugal. The combination of the American disengagement from Indochina and the switch to an

Table 9

NATO AND WARSAW PACT FORCES, BY REGION, 1969 AND 1977

Type of Force	Northern and Central Europe[a]			Southern Europe[b]		
	NATO	Warsaw Pact	[Soviet only]	NATO	Warsaw Pact	[Soviet only]
1969						
Combat and direct support troops available	700,000	925,000	[600,000]	525,000	375,000	[100,000]
Medium/heavy tanks available in peacetime	5,250	12,500	[8,000]	1,800	4,600	[1,300]
Tank/troops ratio	1:133	1:74	[1:75]	1:292	1:82	[1:77]
1977						
Combat manpower in all types of formations	670,000	945,000	[640,000]	560,000	390,000	[145,000]
Main battle tanks in operational service	7,810	20,500	[13,500]	4,000	6,700	[2,500]
Tank/troops ratio	1:86	1:46	[1:47]	1:140	1:58	[1:58]

Source: Institute for Strategic Studies, *The Military Balance, 1969-1970*, pp. 62-63; *1977-1978*, pp. 103-7.

[a]Includes, on the NATO side, Norway, Denmark, Schleswig-Holstein, and NATO forces in the Center Region (the Benelux countries and the rest of the FRG). Also includes those French forces stationed in the FRG and in northeastern France. Does not include allied forces in Portugal or the UK. Includes, on the Warsaw Pact side, Pact forces in the DDR, Czechoslovakia, Poland, and the northern and western military districts of the USSR. It is not possible to judge which Warsaw Pact forces would be directed against NATO's Northern Region (Norway, Denmark, Schleswig-Holstein and the Baltic Approaches) rather than the Center Region, since Warsaw Pact land and air forces are flexible and could be used against both. Northern and Central Europe are thus grouped together.

[b]Includes, on the NATO side, the Italian, Greek, and Turkish forces, plus American and British units that would be committed to the Mediterranean theater. Includes, on the Warsaw Pact side, Bulgarian, Rumanian, and Hungarian forces, plus Soviet forces in Hungary and in the southwestern USSR that might be committed to the Mediterranean theater.

all-volunteer force meant that by 1977 American forces were roughly 20 percent smaller than in the years before the rapid escalation of the war in Vietnam. The U.S. Seventh Army in West Germany was cut back even further during this period, declining from 210,000 in 1968 to 189,000 in 1977.[36]

Even though they had been reducing the size of their armed forces, all of the European members of NATO (again with the exception of Portugal) increased defense spending in real terms between 1968 and 1977 (see Table 10). Defense spending in the United States, by contrast, fell steadily in real terms between 1968 and 1976 to a level only slightly higher than that of 1960. Some of the largest increases during this period were registered by the smaller members of NATO, especially the Netherlands, Belgium, Norway, and Denmark. Over the periods 1960-1970 and 1970-1980, Belgium, the Netherlands, Norway, Denmark, and West Germany all achieved higher average annual increases in defense spending than the United States (see Table 11).

Moreover, the European members of NATO were able to continue to increase defense spending during the 1970s despite a political climate that had become less favorable to such increases. The changed climate was due to three beliefs that came to be widely held in Europe during this period: (1) the Soviet Union did not represent a serious threat to attack Western Europe, (2) the military strength of East and West was about equal, and (3) equality between the blocs was to be preferred to American superiority because equality reduced the risk of war and of an East-West arms race.[37]

This, then, is the political context in which recent complaints by Americans in and out of government about the alleged unwillingness of the European members of NATO to increase defense spending should be evaluated. When in 1977 the Carter administration proposed that the Alliance agree on a Long-Term Defense Program backed by real annual increases in defense spending of about 3 percent, it was not the Europeans who had failed to increase defense spending during the preceding decade but rather the United States. The Alliance has encountered problems in adhering to the plans formulated during 1977 and 1978, but on the whole its actions suggest that the

Table 10

NATO DEFENSE EXPENDITURES, 1960-1979, IN CONSTANT PRICES (1970 = 100)[a]

Country	1960	1968	1969	1970	1971	1972	1973	1974	1975	1976	1977	1978	1979
Belgium	72.5	93.9	94.0	100.0	101.3	107.0	110.9	115.4	124.7	133.4	136.4	144.9	148.2
Britain	100.6	106.9	100.2	100.0	105.2	113.7	112.0	115.9	114.6	116.8	112.1	113.7	117.1
Canada	105.3	101.1	95.2	100.0	100.6	100.8	100.6	108.0	106.6	113.6	121.1	123.9	117.6
Denmark	71.4	103.7	102.0	100.0	109.4	108.9	103.6	113.2	122.9	121.3	122.1	124.7	125.4
France	85.7	102.3	101.1	100.0	99.8	99.2	101.1	108.1	112.5	117.2	123.7	128.4	133.7
West Germany	70.2	91.1	99.2	100.0	107.2	114.6	119.0	124.2	123.6	122.4	121.7	125.8	127.6
Greece	44.2	81.7	92.6	100.0	105.8	112.6	112.9	108.1	172.6	144.1[b]	152.1[b]	153.3[b]	139.3[b]
Italy	67.0	96.8	94.8	100.0	113.1	125.0	124.7	124.8	116.7	115.8	124.1	127.5	135.6
Luxembourg	81.5	96.3	98.3	100.0	101.6	112.9	124.1	133.5	141.8	131.9	148.9	162.8	167.5
Netherlands	65.6	92.0	96.1	100.0	104.7	108.2	110.0	117.9	120.7	119.7	133.2	129.5	137.3
Norway	59.2	94.5	99.8	100.0	102.5	102.6	103.3	106.0	115.0	117.8	120.1	126.6	129.6
Portugal	37.3	98.7	91.0	100.0	104.7	103.3	95.4	114.4	78.6	61.5	58.2	60.9	62.4
Turkey	68.4	93.0	92.6	100.0	114.3	123.6	131.1	147.0	131.9[b]	177.3[b]	222.0[b]	182.3[b]	178.1[b]
United States	76.5	115.7	110.8	100.0	92.3	92.6	88.1	86.9	84.3	79.7	83.0	80.4	80.9

Source: Institute for Strategic Studies, The Military Balance, 1978-1979, p. 87; 1981-1982, p. 110.

[a]Based on the standard NATO definition of defense expenditures.
[b]Based on national—not NATO—definitions of defense expenditure.

Table 11

AVERAGE ANNUAL INCREASES IN DEFENSE SPENDING IN CONSTANT PRICES, 1960-1980

(in percent)

1960-1970[a]		1970-1980[a]		1975-1980[a]	
Portugal	10.4%	Greece	5.88%	Norway	6.78%
Greece	8.5	Luxembourg	4.84	Luxembourg	5.90
Norway	5.4	Belgium	4.29	Greece	4.68
Netherlands	4.3	Norway	4.21	Britain	3.92
Italy	4.1	Italy	3.50[c]	France	3.73
Turkey[b]	3.9	Netherlands	3.38	Belgium	3.70
West Germany	3.6	France	3.00	Canada	3.36
Denmark	3.4	Canada	2.49	Netherlands	2.80
Belgium	3.3	Turkey[b]	2.48	Italy	2.04
United States	2.7	Britain	2.31	West Germany	1.27
Luxembourg	2.1	West Germany	1.51	United States	0.40
France	1.6	Denmark	1.16	Denmark	-1.31
Britain	0	United States	-1.50	Portugal	-6.62
Canada	-0.5	Portugal	-5.65	Turkey[b]	-10.32

Source: Institute for Strategic Studies, *The Military Balance, 1982-1983*, p. 118.

[a] Average annual compound growth rate, based on standard NATO definition of defense spending.

[b] Based on national definition of defense spending.

[c] 1970-1979

23

members of the Alliance—the Europeans as well as the United States—have not lost their ability to take the steps necessary to maintain a military balance in Europe.

For example, as part of an American-proposed package of "quick fixes," during 1977 and 1978 the number of modern antitank guided missiles stockpiled by the NATO countries increased by one-third, ammunition stockpiles were increased, and ammunition supplies were moved forward to improve reaction time in the event of an attack.[38] The United States and West Germany reached agreement on the transfer of an American mechanized brigade to the northern part of the FRG to reduce the disparity between NATO's Northern and Central Army Groups, and American officials moved ahead with plans to increase the amount of equipment pre-positioned in Europe in order to speed the arrival of reinforcements from North America.[39] The Europeans for their part agreed at the May 1979 meeting of the Alliance's Defense Policy Committee that the Alliance would spend $4.5 billion on infrastructure construction between 1980 and 1984 to provide the aircraft shelters, ammunition depots, and reception facilities needed to handle a large flow of reinforcements.[40] The NATO countries also reached agreement to spend about $2 billion to purchase a fleet of 18 AWACS aircraft that would be owned and operated by the Alliance as a whole—the largest acquisition program ever funded by the Alliance.[41]

In 1978 the size of the combined armed forces of the NATO countries increased after declining for nine consecutive years, and the ratio of NATO to Warsaw Pact forces also improved in 1978, again after declining for nine consecutive years (see Appendix). As of 1982, both of these indicators had shown improvement for five consecutive years. Between 1977 and 1982, Belgium, Canada, Greece, Italy, Norway, Portugal, Turkey, West Germany, and the United States all increased the size of their armed forces. During 1981, Spain edged closer to formal membership in the Alliance, and its entry in 1982 made it the first new member since 1955.

Adherence to the commitment to increase defense spending by 3 percent per year in real terms has been mixed. During 1979, the first year to which the commitment was to apply, only half the members of the Alliance increased defense spending by 3 percent or more, based on the standard NATO definition of defense spending (see Table 10). In 1980, only about one-third of the members did so.[42] Norway and the Netherlands, supposedly two of the most advanced cases of the "Dutch disease," met the commitment in both years, as did Luxembourg, whereas the United States fell short in both years. The worldwide economic slowdown during 1981-1982 added to the difficulties of meeting the 3 percent goal, but there appears to have been a genuine effort on the part of most members to meet it. In November 1980, the Dutch defense white paper endorsed the goal and pledged that, with the exception of a "single departure from the 3 percent norm" in 1981, the Netherlands would strive to meet it for the rest of the decade.[43] Also in November 1980, NATO sources in Brussels let it be known that the Alliance was broadly "on target" for an overall increase in defense spending of 3 percent in 1981, with Denmark and Belgium the two main "soft spots."[44] In September 1981, the newly-elected Conservative Party government in Norway committed itself to real annual increases in defense spending of 4 percent, while the new Socialist government in France announced that military spending would increase by 18 percent in 1982.[45] U.S. officials let it be known at the end of 1981 that most NATO countries would meet or come close to the 3 percent goal in 1982.[46]

European Pacifism. Even if the governments of the European members of NATO are able to increase defense spending, will their citizens be willing to fight in defense of their countries? The claim that anti-defense movements are growing in strength in Denmark, Norway, the Netherlands, and West Germany constitutes a crucial link in the argument that the condition of the Alliance is worse now than ever before.[47] Is pacifism spreading in Western Europe? Has it reached the point at which the viability of the Alliance is threatened?

The extent of pacifist sentiment in Western Europe is difficult to measure because a willingness to state that one is prepared to fight in defense of one's country can be significantly influenced by expectations about the nature and outcome of a possible war. Questions in public opinion surveys that omit any reference to the kind of weapons that would be used or to the location of the fighting generally elicit sizable majorities of Western Europeans who would prefer to fight rather than accept Soviet domination (see Table 12).[48] In the case of West Germany, those prepared to fight exceeded those who preferred Soviet domination by a margin of 74 percent to 19. However, when a national sample in West Germany was asked if the FRG should use "military weapons" to defend itself against an attack *on its soil*, the percentage agreeing dropped to 64; 19 percent were opposed. When asked if the FRG should defend itself against a military attack "even if the war is fought primarily on the soil of the FRG," the percentage agreeing dropped even further—to 53; 31 percent were opposed. Only 15 percent were in favor of defense against an attack "if nuclear weapons have to be used on the soil of the FRG"; 71 percent were opposed.[49]

Table 12

Some people say that war is now so horrible that it is better to accept Russian domination than to risk war. Others say it would be better to fight in defense of [name country] than to accept Russian domination. Which opinion is closer to your own?

| | Percent Response | | |
Country	Better to Fight	Better to Be Dominated	Don't Know
Britain	75%	12%	13%
France	57	13	30
FRG	74	19	7
Italy	48	17	35
Belgium	45	14	41
Denmark	51	17	32
United States	83	6	11

Source: Gallup International Research Institutes, May 1982.

Available survey data do not show clearly whether pacifist sentiments have recently been increasing or holding steady in Western Europe. On the one hand, time-series data suggest that a desire to avoid war at all costs rather than use nuclear weapons for defense has increased since the 1950s (see Table 13).[50] The greatest increases of this sort occurred during the 1960s and early 1970s, when the spirit of detente replaced the tensions of the Cold War in Europe. On the other hand, surveys conducted in West Germany in 1954 and 1955 indicated strong opposition even then to the use of nuclear weapons in response to a non-nuclear attack (see Table 14).[51]

Table 13

If we should someday face the choice either of allowing Europe to become sovietized or to defend ourselves against the Russians with all possible means, which would you consider more important: to defend our way of life [1976: democratic freedom] even if it should result in a nuclear war, or to do everything possible to avoid war, even if this would mean living under a communist government?

	Year/Percent Response: West Germany								
Response	1955	1956	1959	1960	1975	1976	1979	May 1981	July 1981
Avoid war	36%	34%	33%	38%	49%	52%	52%	48%	45%
Defend our way of life	33	35	32	30	25	28	23	27	30
Impossible to say	31	31	35	32	26	20	25	25	25

Source: Allensbach Institute for Demoscopy.

Table 14

Supposing Russia were to attack West Germany without using atomic weapons: would you personally then agree to America's using atomic and hydrogen bombs on Russia in order to defend West Germany, or wouldn't you?

Response	Date/Percent Response: West Germany	
	April 1954	September 1955
Would agree to using A- and H-weapons	22%	15%
Would not agree	60	65
No opinion	18	20

Source: Hans Speier, *German Rearmament and Atomic War*, p. 253.

Strong opposition to the use of nuclear weapons for defense is by no means found only among European publics. In a May 1982 survey, only one-fourth of American respondents thought the United States would be justified using nuclear weapons first in a war. Only 28 percent thought the United States would be justified using nuclear weapons first to stop a Soviet attack on Western Europe.[52]

It is important to distinguish between an aversion to defense strategies based on nuclear weapons and an aversion to military preparedness. Time-series data on Dutch and West German attitudes suggest that the percentage believing a military counterbalance is necessary to offset Soviet power declined only slightly between 1974 and 1982 (see Table 15).[53] More important, even among Dutch

Table 15

Do you believe a military counterbalance to be necessary in Western Europe to offset the power of Russia and the other countries of Eastern Europe, or do you consider this unnecessary?

	Date/Percent Response: The Netherlands						
Response	July 1974	Nov. 1974	Oct. 1979	Jan. 1980	Dec. 1980	Oct. 1981	Jan. 1982
Necessary	68%	66%	67%	65%	68%	65%	67%
Unnecessary	15	24	21	22	21	19	22
No answer	17	10	12	13	11	16	11

Source: Netherlands Institute of Public Opinion.

If someone said that an attack from the East could best be prevented by deterrence when the West was itself adequately armed, would you agree with him or not?

	Date/Percent Response: West Germany				
	February 1976	January 1978	September 1979	March 1981	July 1981
Agree	58%	58%	55%	50%	53%
Disagree	23	22	21	25	22
No opinion	19	20	24	25	25

Source: Allensbach Institute for Demoscopy.

respondents who felt their chances of personal survival were "zero or very small" in the event of a war in Europe, sizable majorities agreed that it was better to defend the Netherlands against a Soviet attack than to capitulate (see Table 16).[54]

Table 16

A. *It is sometimes said that war would now be so terrible that it would be better not to resist an attacker—that is, not defend the Netherlands but capitulate. Do you or don't you agree with that?*

B. *Which would you choose in the worst possible situation: to allow a Russian occupation of the Netherlands or to defend ourselves with all the dangerous consequences?*

| | Percent Response | |
| | If chances of survival in case of war in Europe including Holland were: | |
Responses	Zero or very small	Not great or great
A. Defend country	61%	76%
Better to surrender	32	21
No opinion	7	3
B. Defend with all consequences	67	81
Allow Russian occupation	25	16
No opinion	8	3

Source: Netherlands Institute of Public Opinion, September 1981.

The data in Tables 13-16 suggest that many West Europeans continue to be willing to use conventional weapons to defend their countries against a Soviet attack—or at least they say they are willing when queried in public opinion polls. A majority of the public in West Germany is unwilling to see the FRG defended if such a defense involves the use of nuclear weapons on German soil, and large segments of the publics in the Netherlands and Britain are opposed to the presence of nuclear weapons in their countries.[55] In other words, pacifism does not appear to be widespread in Western Europe in the sense that many West Europeans would refuse to fight under any circumstances, but many West Europeans are unwilling to resort to weapons that could result in the annihilation of their homelands.

It is important to place these sentiments in historical perspective. The apparent spread of "nuclear pacifism" in Western Europe during the 1970s was not the first time that Western European publics have rebelled against defense strategies that seemed to promise annihilation rather than protection. In West Germany during the early 1950s, proposals for German rearmament were greeted by many young West Germans with a combination of fear, derision, and even violence. Creation of a West German army seemed to many young West Germans as but the first step in a repetition of the events of the 1930s that had led to disaster:

> Nearly every young German—whether drafted at seventeen, or an "anti-aircraft helper" at fifteen, or only a little boy of ten sitting out the bombings in cellars at night—has traumatic memories of war, and these memories are associated with the image of a militarized Germany, or more exactly, of a German army. A 1944 snapshot of a young boy in a Luftwaffe uniform weeping in despair has been reprinted by several German magazines as a powerful reminder.[56]

These sentiments were coupled with a belief that a future war would irreparably devastate Germany and result in the slaughter of millions of its citizens. Such a war would be waged exclusively in the interests of others, although Germans would inevitably bear the brunt of the fighting.[57]

Polls taken at the time found strong sentiments against rearmament. In a December 1950 poll conducted for the U.S. State Department, only 30 percent of West German respondents approved of rearmament, and only 7 percent indicated willingness to serve.[58] Opposition to German rearmament was reduced somewhat by the prospective integration of German soldiers into the supra-national army planned for the European Defense Community (EDC). In a December 1953 poll, before the rejection of the EDC treaty by France, 28 percent of young West Germans said they would refuse to serve under any conditions, although nearly half said they would be willing to serve "under certain conditions." In November 1954, after the French rejection of the treaty, the percentage of young Germans saying they would refuse to serve under any conditions increased to 44.[59] Attempts by officials of the future West German defense ministry to explain the reforms and safeguards that were to be incorporated into the new German army were shouted down by hostile audiences. When Theodor Blank, the first West German Commissioner of Security, spoke in Augsburg during a Bavarian state election campaign, "beer steins and soft drink bottles were thrown at him. He abandoned the attempt to speak, and as he emerged bleeding from the meeting hall he was again attacked and beaten by young demonstrators."[60]

The Adenauer government sought to counter the opposition to rearmament by arguing that it was the price of regaining German sovereignty and ending the Allied occupation. It also sought to foster the notion that a German army and entry into NATO would prevent Germany from again suffering the horrors of war. As Gordon Craig has noted, the German people

> were encouraged by government spokesmen to believe that adhesion to a European coalition would somehow or other make possible a "forward strategy" so effective that West Germany would be spared the horrors of being a battlefield. In July 1952 CDU Deputy Strauss said: "We expect of the Federal Government that it will press successfully for a strategic concept in which Germany cannot become the theater of conflict." Between that time and the end of 1954, the government intimated frequently that it was assured of this happy immunity. Indeed, as late as March 1955, Chancellor Adenauer had no hesitation in stating flatly, "So long as we do not belong to NATO we are, in the case of a hot war between Soviet Russia and the United States, the European battlefield; and if we are in the Atlantic Pact Organization, then we are no longer that battlefield."[61]

The Adenauer government's efforts were not helped by the December 1954 decision by the North Atlantic Council to base the

Alliance's future strategic plans on the assumption that nuclear weapons would be used to defend against a Soviet attack. West German opponents of rearmament questioned the value of 500,000 German soldiers if any future war was to be fought from the start with nuclear weapons.[62] Others argued that the NATO decision meant that Germany would be the battlefield upon which atomic weapons would be exploded in the event of a Soviet attack. Proponents of this argument received an unexpected assist from Operation Carte Blanche—a NATO air exercise conducted in June 1955 in which 335 simulated nuclear explosions were set off in the area between Hamburg and Munich, resulting in an estimated 1.7 million Germans killed and 3.5 million wounded, not counting casualties from radiation. Press accounts of the exercise appeared at virtually the same time that the Bundestag was being asked to approve the Volunteers Bill, which would authorize an initial cadre of 6,000 soldiers for the new German army.[63]

Whatever its purpose, the principal effects of Operation Carte Blanche were to intimidate the German people and embarrass the Adenauer government.[64] Opposition spokesmen scornfully recalled the Chancellor's promises that entry into NATO would spare the Federal Republic the horrors of being a battlefield. Theodor Blank insisted that the Carte Blanche exercise did not prove that the destructive power of atomic bombs made ground forces unnecessary, because tests in the Nevada desert had shown that well-protected troops could survive atomic attacks. When asked by one opposition deputy, "Where are we going to get the deserts?," the Security Commissioner chose not to answer.[65] Other government spokesmen sought to dispose of the awkward December 1954 Council decision by denying its existence or suggesting that it would be changed. On the whole, the Adenauer government was able to weather this storm and press ahead with its plans for rearmament because it had a well-disciplined parliamentary majority rather than because it offered persuasive arguments.[66]

When conscription was enacted into law in 1956, opposition to the Adenauer government's rearmament plans spread rapidly. Even within the government parties, Blank's plans for an 18-month term of service were severely criticized, and in September 1956 the Cabinet announced that the term of military service for conscripts would be set at 12 months. The Cabinet's decision coincided with reports in both the German and foreign press that the Adenauer government was planning to request that the Bundeswehr be equipped with tactical nuclear weapons to compensate for the manpower shortage that would result from the shortened term of service. (The warheads would remain in American custody.)[67] In the meantime, discussion in the press of the Adenauer government's plans caused a considerable uproar in the Federal Republic. At the December 1956 meeting of the North Atlantic Council, the British took the lead in suggesting that American tactical nuclear weapons be made available to the European members of NATO. Nuclear sharing was formally agreed upon at the December 1957 meeting of the Council—a decision that "brought public feeling [in the FRG] to a head and touched off the public debate on atomic weapons that raged during the first six months of 1958 and exceeded in violence any previous public discussions of strategy questions."[68]

At first, criticism of Adenauer's plans came primarily from opposition Social Democrat (SPD) deputies in the Bundestag, who strongly disapproved of the plans during the parliamentary debate on defense in the spring of 1957. The SPD also made the Chancellor's plans a key issue in the national election of November 1957. That election resulted in an absolute majority for Adenauer's Christian Democrat (CDU/CSU) party, and in March 1958 the Chancellor presented his defense program to the Bundestag for approval. SPD members sought to circumvent the CDU majority in the Bundestag by organizing a campaign for statewide popular referenda on the question of atomic weapons for the Bundeswehr. The Adenauer government was able to secure injunctions from the Supreme Court in May 1958 forbidding such referenda, but by then the principal source of opposition to Adenauer's plans was a grassroots protest movement—the Kampf dem Atomtod (Struggle Against Atomic Death).[69] The five-month-long Kampf dem Atomtod movement involved petition-signing campaigns as well as mass public protests during which hundreds of thousands of demonstrators took to the streets to express their disapproval of the government's defense policies. Participants included SPD members, trade unionists, students, and church representatives. The movement continued throughout the summer of 1958, although SPD support diminished after the CDU won an absolute majority in the July state elections in North Rhine-land/Westphalia, which the SPD had sought to make into a referendum on atomic weapons and support for NATO.

THE ALLIANCE AND ITS CRISES

Judgments about the relative severity of different NATO crises and thus about whether the condition of the Alliance is worse now than ever before are very difficult to make with confidence. While there are important similarities between the recent protests and demonstrations in Europe and the protests of the 1950s, there are also important differences. Some of these differences point toward the conclusion that the current anti-nuclear movement constitutes a much more formidable threat to the viability of the Alliance than earlier movements like the Kampf dem Atomtod. But other differences suggest that the current anti-nuclear movement may lack the breadth of support and intensity of feeling that characterized the protests of the 1950s.

As in the case of the protests of the 1950s, the current anti-nuclear movement appears strongest in West Germany—then as now the most important European member of NATO. As in the 1950s, the most active participants in the current protests have been students and young people, although in both cases the protests have been more than just a youth movement, involving representatives of the trade unions, churches, and socialist parties.

Perhaps the most obvious difference between the current protests and those of the 1950s is the broader scope of the current movement. As Stanley Hoffmann has noted, the current movement "is a mass movement of continental dimensions, which mobilizes and moves people across borders."[70] The protest movements of the 1950s tended to be confined within single countries—particularly West Germany and Britain. It is the transnational nature of the current anti-nuclear movement, and especially the emergence of sizable and well-organized anti-nuclear groups in many European countries at the same time, that has contributed more than anything else to the impression that the recent protests confront the Alliance with the most serious crisis it has ever faced.

And yet there are other differences between the recent protests and those of the 1950s which suggest that the recent opposition to NATO's proposed missile deployments may not be as formidable a challenge to the viability of the Alliance as the earlier protest movements. In the case of the opposition to German rearmament during the early 1950s, opinion polls at the time suggested that there was widespread opposition in West Germany to an army of any kind or to any foreign policy that seemed to involve a heightened risk of fighting on German soil. The protest movement of the 1980s has been more narrowly focused on the Alliance's plans for new continental-range nuclear missiles and the danger of nuclear war in Europe, with large majorities in West Germany and other West European states continuing to favor a conventional defense of Western Europe.

Similarly, at least in West Germany, the opposition to the Alliance's plans appears to be more narrowly based than were earlier protest movements. In a February 1958 poll, the deployment of nuclear weapons delivery systems in West Germany was opposed by 81 percent of West German respondents.[71] The percentage of West German respondents expressing opposition to the Alliance's plans to deploy new nuclear missiles in Europe can vary considerably, depending on the wording of the questions used in opinion polls, but on the whole such opposition does not appear as extensive as in the 1950s. In a May 1981 poll, when asked if they favored the deployment of new long-range missiles on German soil, 39 percent of West German respondents said they were opposed to such deployment, while only 29 percent said they were in favor (32 percent were undecided). When asked if new NATO missiles should be installed to counterbalance Soviet missiles, the percentage supporting such a plan increased to 37, with 33 percent opposed. When the proposed missile deployment was linked to the objective of securing an arms control agreement with the Soviets, 53 percent responded that this was a good idea, while only 20 percent said it was a bad idea.[72]

On balance, the current controversy over deploying new continental-range nuclear missiles in Europe does not appear to be unprecedented or fundamentally different from earlier controversies over the role of nuclear weapons in the Alliance's strategy. Claims that the condition of the Alliance is worse now than ever before or that there is a "basic trend" pulling Americans and Europeans apart on the whole appear exaggerated. Neutralist sentiment in Western Europe appears to be no more widespread now than in earlier years. The publics in the countries of Western Europe are deeply concerned about the risk of nuclear war and the role of nuclear weapons in Alliance strategy, but this is a long-standing concern rather than a recent or novel development. And the governments of the states of Western Europe have not lost the ability to take the steps needed to balance Soviet power—at least not yet.

As these carefully hedged conclusions suggest, there is a limit to how far judgments concerning the condition of the Alliance can be pushed. An ability to surmount past crises offers no guarantee that the Alliance will be able to surmount future crises. To say that predictions of the Alliance's imminent demise appear unwarranted is not to establish that the Alliance is in sound shape and can be expected to remain that way indefinitely. The evidence presented here shows only that much recent commentary on the state of the Alliance has lacked historical perspective and thus has been based on exaggerated notions of the problems now confronting the Alliance.

Reports of widespread disarray and imminent disintegration, if repeated often enough by enough observers, may eventually be taken seriously both by elites and by the publics in member states. Hence it is important to expose exaggerated claims for what they are, lest the result be a self-fulfilling prophecy.

But even though the Alliance has demonstrated an ability to survive past crises, and even if the current Alliance crisis is not unprecedented, this in no way proves that the Alliance will endure indefinitely. It doesn't even prove that the Alliance will survive the current crisis. Hence it is important to probe the history of previous Alliance crises to see what can be learned from them about how to manage—and if possible, avoid—crises within the Alliance.

II

THE ATLANTIC ALLIANCE AND LRTNF:
WAS THIS CRISIS NECESSARY?

NATO crises over the role of nuclear weapons in the Alliance's strategy have often been analyzed in terms of the concepts of "coupling" and "decoupling." That is, the source of previous crises has often been traced to European fears about the credibility of the American nuclear guarantee—especially to European concern that the United States would seek to "decouple" its strategic deterrent from Europe in order to preserve the United States as a sanctuary from Soviet nuclear retaliation in the event NATO used nuclear weapons to respond to a Soviet attack in Europe. The recent crisis over the Alliance's plans to deploy new continental-range nuclear missiles in Europe has brought these concerns to the fore once again. Opponents of the Alliance's December 1979 decision have argued that deployment of the Pershings and the ground-launched cruise missiles would in effect "decouple" the American strategic deterrent from Europe by allowing the United States to strike the Soviet Union with missiles based in Europe, making possible a nuclear war confined to Europe. Proponents of the new missiles have viewed their deployment very differently, arguing that the effect would be to "couple" the American strategic deterrent more tightly to Europe than ever before, since the Soviet Union would almost certainly respond against the homeland of the owner of a nuclear weapon exploded on Soviet territory rather than the site from which the warhead was launched, thereby activating American strategic nuclear forces.

That the discussion of previous Alliance crises has proceeded in this fashion should come as no surprise. Ever since the formation of the Alliance, the United States has sought to deter the Soviets and reassure its European allies by threatening to retaliate against a Soviet attack in Europe with the full spectrum of forces available to it. But in view of the obvious risks associated with striking the Soviet Union with nuclear weapons once the Soviets had developed the means to retaliate directly against the United States, it was practically a foregone conclusion that the European members of NATO would never be wholly persuaded by these American pledges to retaliate. No matter how often they are repeated, the Europeans will always be tempted to suspect that the United States is secretly looking for ways to avoid bringing down Soviet retaliation upon itself. Suggestions that the proposed deployment of the Pershings and the ground-launched cruise missiles can be rendered unnecessary by "unequivocal reassurances of the American guarantee to Europe"[73] are specious; regardless of how forcefully these pledges are made, there will always be some in Europe who will question them. These doubts will exist as long as there are 3,000 miles of ocean separating Europe from America.

This is not to say nothing can be done to reduce tensions within the Alliance over nuclear weapons issues. It is evident from the earlier discussion that Europeans have on the whole welcomed the Alliance and the link with the United States because it has provided more security against the threat of Soviet attack or intimidation than they could possibly muster on their own. Yet Europeans and Americans alike have never been able to concentrate solely on their common interest in deterring a Soviet attack and to ignore how their interests would diverge in the event deterrence failed. Just as Americans have been ambivalent about the risk entailed by a nuclear guarantee to Europe by the United States, so too have Europeans been ambivalent about the risk of entanglement in clashes between the superpowers. Just as American administrations have sought to build "firebreaks" that would reduce the risk that a conflict in Europe would automatically escalate to a central strategic exchange between the United States and the Soviet Union, so too have the European members of the Alliance been tempted by the notion that Europe can somehow avoid being dragged into what are essentially quarrels between the United States and the Soviet Union. Just as the American view on the risk of "coupling" the American strategic deterrent to Europe has been shaped by the geographical separation of America from Europe, so too have European views on the need to insulate Europe from the quarrels of the superpowers been shaped by structural influences—namely, the attempt by a group of middle and small powers to seek protection from one superpower by enlisting the aid of the other. The essence of the problem from the European point of view was apparent even before the North Atlantic Treaty had been signed, as illustrated by a comment by French Foreign Minister Bidault to the American ambassador in Paris:

> In the long run if war comes, the victory on your side is certain, but what will happen to us in the meantime? We know that you will do your best, but what can I say to my critics who do not want to see France overrun by the Russians?[74]

As a result of these concerns, the European members of the Alliance have often looked to it to provide more than merely the promise of American support in the event of war. That is, they have sought from the Alliance not only a guarantee of their security, but also a virtual guarantee of immunity from war itself. The preceding section suggests that whenever it has appeared that the Alliance could not provide such a guarantee, or whenever it has appeared that the Alliance's strategy for meeting a Soviet attack would likely involve the destruction of what was to be defended, European publics have been tempted to rebel against the Alliance—as in the case of the strong opposition within the Federal Republic to German rearmament or the Kampf dem Atomtod. This yearning for a guarantee of immunity against attack helps explain why the Adenauer government responded to the protests of the 1950s with extravagant claims about the ability of the Alliance to prevent Germany from ever again becoming a battlefield.

Viewed from this perspective, the protests and demonstrations in Europe in 1981 and 1982 appear neither unprecedented nor surprising. They are instead best understood as the latest manifestation of long-standing fears that the Alliance's strategy—and especially its reliance on nuclear weapons—would lead to the destruction of what

the Alliance was created to defend. The recurrence of mass demonstrations and protests in Europe after a period of nearly two decades
of relative calm on defense issues is perhaps best explained in terms
of the intersection of two currents of opinion. On the one hand, as
of March 1981, "majorities in West Germany, Italy, the Netherlands,
and Norway were *not* concerned that the Soviet Union would 'attack
Western Europe within the next five years.' Opinion in France and
Britain was about evenly divided."[75] On the other hand, concern
that the likelihood of war was increasing itself increased in Europe
during the 1970s despite the growing movement toward detente (see
Table 17).[76] The intersection of these two currents of opinion was

Table 17

*Here is a sort of scale. Would you, with the help of this card, tell me how you
assess the chances of a world war breaking out in the next ten years?* [Scale grad-
uated in tens from 100 = "War certain" to 0 = "No risk of war"]

Percent Responding More than 50-50 Chance of War in Next 10 Years by Country

Date	Belgium	Denmark	FRG	France	Italy	Netherlands	Britain
July 1971	8%	—	11%	12%	13%	11%	—
Oct/Nov 1977	21	10%	13	14	14	17	13%
April 1980	33	18	25	42	32	24	39
October 1981	32	—	32	25	18	20	21

Source: Euro-barometre, No. 16, December 1981.

perhaps best captured in a seven-country survey in October 1982
which presented respondents with a list of ten problems and asked
them to identify "your greatest concerns for yourself and your country today." The "threat of war" was the third most frequently cited
problem (behind crime and unemployment), chosen by an average of
35 percent of the respondents in the seven countries surveyed.
"Inadequate defense," in contrast, was ranked last, selected by an
average of only 7 percent of the respondents polled.[77]

The result of the intersection of these two currents of opinion was to resurrect a fear that had first appeared in West Germany more than a quarter-century earlier. The fear is not so much of a specific, identifiable threat from the Soviet Union, which has usually resulted in closer links between the United States and its European allies. Instead, the concerns that motivated the protests and demonstrations of 1981 and 1982 were more diffuse. Just as young West Germans in the early 1950s feared that German rearmament would inevitably embroil Germany in a war fought primarily for the interests of others, so too did many young West Europeans in the early 1980s fear that their fate was in the hands of others, and that Europe could be devastated by a conflict that started outside of Europe but would inevitably spread to Europe. The LRTNF decision was a catalyst that brought to the surface fears that had been building for some time.

The fears that were crystallized by the LRTNF decision did not mean that the Alliance was no longer valued by Europeans or that the American presence in Europe was no longer desired. The data presented earlier suggest that large majorities in the countries of Western Europe still consider the Alliance essential for their security. There is no inconsistency between support for the Alliance and for the presence of American troops in Europe and skepticism about the Alliance's plans to install new nuclear missiles in Europe. West Germans, as Werner Kaltefleiter has noted, recognize "their vulnerability in the event of an American troop withdrawal; if the nation were then subjected to a surprise attack, West Germans are convinced by a three-to-one margin that they would be overrun."[78] The protests and demonstrations in 1981 and 1982 were a reminder of fears and emotions that have always been present in Western Europe and which come to the surface whenever the Alliance seems to veer away from the function of providing security and reassurance to Europeans in favor of focusing on nuclear war-fighting, targetting options, and so on.

There is an inherent dilemma in this respect that the Alliance will never be able to avoid entirely. One way to alleviate the tensions and fears brought to the surface by the LRTNF decision would be for the NATO countries to refrain from discussing nuclear weapons

41

issues in public, but this is impossible for an alliance of democratic states. Once these issues are discussed in public, it may be difficult if not impossible to design a military posture and declaratory policy that frightens the Soviets enough to deter them without causing substantial anxiety among the publics of Western Europe.[79]

This suggests that many of the tensions and strains that have recently troubled the Alliance stem from failure to recall why the Alliance was formed and why it has endured. Except for a brief period in 1950 and 1951, few government officials on either side of the Atlantic have regarded a massive Soviet attack on Western Europe as a serious possibility. Instead, the contest in Europe has been viewed as a political-psychological one, in which the principal threat has been Soviet efforts to use the fear of war and its consequences to coerce or intimidate the countries of Western Europe.[80] The purpose of the Alliance was not so much to coordinate war plans as to provide a visible sign of American support, which was considered crucial for stiffening European resolve sufficiently to enable the countries of Western Europe to resist Soviet political pressures and intimidation.

The United States has an interest in steering discussions of the role of nuclear weapons in the Alliance's strategy away from war-fighting scenarios and the concepts of "coupling" and "decoupling." It serves neither American nor Alliance interests to suggest that an American President would find it easier to fire nuclear missiles at the Soviet Union if they were based in Europe rather than in the United States. To convey that impression, which is implied in the argument that the Pershings and the ground-launched cruise missiles will "couple" the American strategic deterrent more tightly to Europe, is to heighten European fears that a goal of American policy is to limit nuclear wars to Europe. It also provides the Soviets with a potent propaganda tool to use in their efforts to split the Alliance.[81]

Contingency plans, targetting options, and war-fighting doctrines may be useful for demonstrating there is substance to the Alliance as well as symbolism, provided they are kept in perspective. As the LRTNF crisis demonstrates, too many war-fighting options can be a liability.[82] A proliferation of doctrines and options may only frighten the people the Alliance was intended to reassure.

By the same logic, it is a mistake to exaggerate Soviet advantages in tanks and combat units while denigrating the Alliance's conventional forces, thus implying there may be no alternative to early and massive use of nuclear weapons should deterrence fail. Recent events in Poland suggest that Soviet lines of communication in that country could be secured in the event of war only by garrisoning the country with large numbers of Soviet troops to guard against sabotage and uprisings there.[83] NATO military commanders have often decried the forces placed at their disposal in their efforts to demonstrate that more is needed, and their complaints and misgivings have often been played prominently in the press. Less attention has been paid to their assessments of what they could do with the forces available to them in the event war occurred. In a 1981 interview, for example, the NATO Supreme Allied Commander in Europe, General Bernard Rogers, was confident that his forces would be able to engage Soviet second-echelon forces in the event of an attack, which "will then be taken under fire and destroyed." When that happened, and the East Europeans faced the prospect of a Western counterattack, "they will be a hell of a lot less faithful to Russia," he insisted.[84]

Finally, essential to the goal of reassuring the publics of Western Europe is a sound military posture. Military solutions will never completely resolve political problems, but a sound military posture can be helpful in alleviating some of the fears that have risen to the surface in Western Europe in recent years. If the Alliance is to endure, its overriding goal should be to prevent wars—not to fight them; beyond that, it should strive to deny to the Soviets the political leverage that would come from obvious superiority in either nuclear or conventional forces.[85] This means that the Alliance's military forces should be organized for deterrence rather than for nuclear war-fighting. It also means that the Alliance should seek to avoid a military posture that would tempt preemption. Finally, it should strive to avoid a military posture or strategic concept that would require early use of nuclear weapons in the unlikely event of war in Europe.

It is essential to bear in mind that there has never been a convincing military rationale for the deployment of new continental-range nuclear missiles in Europe—there are no targets that cannot be covered equally well by American strategic nuclear forces based in the United States or on submarines patrolling near Europe. The rationale for the deployment of new long-range missiles in Europe is a political one: to deny the Soviets any leverage they might be able to derive from a theoretical ability to exploit weaknesses in the chain of NATO deterrent forces ranging from conventional forces to theater nuclear forces in Europe to American strategic nuclear forces. As Soviet pressures to stop the planned missile deployments become more intense, even that rationale becomes secondary to proving that the Alliance can act in unison in the face of Soviet objections and that it can take the politically distasteful steps necessary to counter Soviet deployments.

The political nature of the rationale for the LRTNF deployments makes it particularly important that the Alliance not become locked into a course that frightens and alienates the very people the Alliance is intended to reassure. This suggests several guidelines for structuring the Alliance's nuclear forces:

First, in the category of LRTNF, the Alliance should rely on cruise missiles supplemented by aircraft on quick-reaction alert rather than Pershing II ballistic missiles. Aircraft and cruise missiles, both with relatively long flight-times to their targets, do not have the first-strike connotations of the Pershings, which would reach Soviet targets within 6-8 minutes of launching.[86]

Second, the cruise missiles deployed by the Alliance should be sea-based rather than land-based to the extent possible. The December 1979 Council decision, which called for a mixed force of land-based Pershings and cruise missiles, was justified in part on the grounds that land-basing was required as a tangible sign of the American commitment. In view of the anxieties aroused by the LRTNF program, this kind of symbol is both unnecessary and unwelcome. The presence of 300,000 American military personnel and their dependents in Europe provides tangible evidence of American support without the threatening implications of the Pershings. Land-basing only reminds the publics of Western Europe of the extent to which their countries can become special targets for Soviet nuclear attack while providing incentives to the Soviets to use barrage tactics in a preemptive strike blanketing the dispersal areas for the land-based missiles. Sea-basing reduces the vulnerability of the Alliance's LRTNF as well as the number of potential targets for a Soviet preemptive strike.

Finally, the Alliance's nuclear forces should be restructured to place greater reliance on long-range theater forces, which are less vulnerable to preemption because they can be based farther from the front. The Alliance's current posture, in which 6,000 or so tactical nuclear warheads are stored in peacetime at about 50 bases (200-300 wartime dispersal sites) is a posture that virtually invites preemption.[87] Sea-basing would permit greater dispersal than the land-basing mode currently planned, and would thus increase the survivability of theater nuclear forces based in Europe.

Changes of this kind will never completely eliminate the fears and anxieties felt in Europe concerning nuclear weapons and their role in the Alliance's strategy, but by emphasizing the extent to which the Alliance is committed to preventing wars rather than fighting them, they can make it easier for the Alliance to perform the function of reassuring the publics of Western Europe rather than frightening them.

CONCLUSION

Questions relating to military preparedness and the measures required for deterrence and defense are among the most sensitive and difficult issues that democratic societies are called on to resolve. The complexities inherent in anticipating the nature of future conflicts and the burdens of preparing for them make it all but inevitable that the NATO countries will disagree on the kinds of programs and the level of effort required for the common defense. The democratic nature of the states that comprise the Alliance makes it all but certain that these disagreements will spill out into the public arena.

In an alliance of democratic societies, disagreements over defense issues are likely to be the norm rather than the exception. Not every disagreement constitutes a crisis, although observers of the Alliance's

45

affairs have been remarkably quick to pronounce the Alliance "in crisis" and even on the brink of disintegration. Perhaps the shrill quality of recent warnings that this time the fatal crisis really is at hand is due in part to the failure of so many previous prophecies of impending collapse to be borne out by events.

Earlier in this paper it has been suggested that the conventional wisdom about the Alliance is wrong. The claims that the condition of the Alliance is worse now than ever before are lacking in historical perspective, and the impressionistic evidence on which such claims are based is hardly an adequate basis for judging whether changes for the worse really are occurring—even less for comparing the relative severity of different Alliance crises. A comparison of the condition of the Alliance at the start of the 1980s with earlier periods in its history suggests that neutralist and pacifist sentiments are not spreading rapidly in Western Europe, that the publics of the countries of Western Europe have not turned against the Alliance or their link with the United States, and that the governments of those countries have not grown passive and defeatist in the face of increasing Soviet power. There are tensions and strains among the members of the Alliance, but on the whole its condition does not appear to be significantly worse now than during earlier periods of crisis. It serves no useful purpose to downplay those tensions and strains, but neither does it serve any constructive purpose to exaggerate them.

Appendix

NATO AND WARSAW PACT
ACTIVE-DUTY ARMED FORCES,
1960-1982

NATO AND WARSAW PACT ACTIVE-DUTY ARMED FORCES, 1960-1982

NATO	1960	1961	1962	1963	1964	1965	1966	1967
Belgium	120,000	110,000	110,000	110,000	110,000	107,000	107,000	102,000
Canada	120,000	119,300	124,000	124,000	120,000	120,000	107,000	103,000
Denmark	44,000	43,000	46,500	49,000	52,000	51,000	50,000	45,500
France	1,026,000	1,008,791	705,000	636,000	620,000	557,000	522,500	520,000
West Germany	260,000	330,000	353,000	404,000	430,000	438,000	440,000	460,000
Greece	157,000	159,000	160,000	160,000	162,000	160,000	159,000	158,000
Italy	400,000	466,392	470,000	470,000	480,000	390,000	376,000	416,000
Luxembourg	3,200[a]	5,500[a]	5,500[a]	5,500[a]	5,500[a]	5,500[a]	1,545	800
Netherlands	135,000	142,000	141,000	141,000	123,500	135,000	129,250	130,000
Norway	40,000	37,000	34,000	36,000	37,000	32,300	34,000	35,000
Portugal	79,000	80,000	80,000	102,000	108,500	148,000	148,000	148,500
Turkey	500,000	500,000	455,000	452,000	480,100	442,000	450,000	480,000
United Kindgom	593,000	454,300	445,000	429,000	425,000	440,000	437,600	429,000
United States	2,489,000	2,606,000	2,815,000	2,700,000	2,690,000	2,660,000	3,093,960	3,400,000
Total	5,967,100	6,061,013	5,944,000	5,829,500	5,843,600	5,685,700	6,055,855	6,427,800
Percent Change		+1.6%	-1.9%	-1.9%	+0.2%	-2.7%	+6.5%	+6.1%
U.S. Share	41.7%	43.0%	47.4%	46.3%	46.0%	46.8%	51.1%	52.9%

Warsaw Pact	1960	1961	1962	1963	1964	1965	1966	1967
Soviet Union	3,623,000	3,800,000	3,600,000	3,300,000	3,300,000	3,150,000	3,165,000	3,220,000
Rumania	200,000	222,000	222,000	227,000	222,000	198,000	201,000	173,000
Poland	200,000	255,000	257,000	257,000	272,000	277,000	260,000	270,000
Czechoslovakia	150,000	185,000	185,000	185,000	235,000	235,000	220,000	225,000
Bulgaria	100,000	120,000	120,000	135,000	150,000	152,000	156,000	154,000
East Germany	65,000	100,000	85,000	116,000	106,000	112,000	122,000	127,000
Hungary	75,000	80,500	80,500	99,000	104,000	109,000	109,000	102,000
Total	4,413,000	4,762,500	4,549,500	4,462,500	4,389,000	4,233,000	4,233,000	4,271,000
Percent Change		+7.9%	-4.5%	-1.9%	-1.6%	-3.6%	----	+0.9%
NATO/Pact Ratio	1.35:1	1.27:1	1.31:1	1.31:1	1.33:1	1.34:1	1.43:1	1.50:1

NATO AND WARSAW PACT ACTIVE-DUTY ARMED FORCES, 1960-1982 (continued)

NATO	1968	1969	1970	1971	1972	1973	1974	1975
Belgium	99,000	102,400	94,000	96,500	90,200	89,600	89,700	87,000
Canada	101,600	98,300	93,325	85,000	84,000	83,000	83,000	77,000
Denmark	45,500	45,500	44,500	40,500	43,400	39,800	37,100	34,400
France	505,000	503,000	506,000	501,500	500,600	503,600	502,500	502,500
West Germany	450,000	465,000	466,000	467,000	467,000	475,000	490,000	495,000
Greece	161,000	159,000	159,000	159,000	157,000	160,000	161,200	161,200
Italy	365,000	420,000	413,000	414,000	427,600	427,500	421,000	421,000
Luxembourg	560	560	550	550	550	550	550	550
Netherlands	128,500	124,000	121,250	116,500	122,200	112,200	113,900	112,500
Norway	35,000	38,000	41,100	35,900	35,900	35,400	34,900	35,000
Portugal	182,500	182,000	185,500	218,000	218,000	204,000	217,000	217,000
Turkey	514,000	483,000	477,500	508,500	449,000	455,000	453,000	453,000
United Kingdom	427,000	405,000	390,000	380,900	372,300	361,500	354,600	345,100
United States	3,500,000	3,454,000	3,161,000	2,699,000	2,391,000	2,252,900	2,174,000	2,130,000
Total	6,520,660	6,479,760	6,102,725	5,722,850	5,358,750	5,200,050	5,132,450	5,071,250
Percent Change	+1.4%	-0.6%	-5.9%	-6.3%	-6.4%	-3.0%	-1.3%	-1.2%
U.S. Share	53.7%	53.3%	51.8%	57.2%	44.6%	43.3%	42.4%	42.0%

Warsaw Pact	1968	1969	1970	1971	1972	1973	1974	1975
Soviet Union	3,220,000	3,300,000	3,305,000	3,375,000	3,375,000	3,425,000	3,525,000	3,575,000
Rumania	173,000	193,000	181,000	160,000	179,000	170,000	171,000	171,000
Poland	274,000	275,000	242,000	265,000	274,000	280,000	303,000	293,000
Czechoslovakia	225,000	230,000	168,000	185,000	185,000	190,000	200,000	200,000
Bulgaria	153,000	154,000	149,000	148,000	146,000	152,000	152,000	152,000
East Germany	126,000	137,000	129,000	126,000	131,000	132,000	145,000	143,000
Hungary	102,000	97,000	101,500	103,000	103,000	103,000	103,000	105,000
Total	4,273,000	4,386,000	4,275,000	4,362,000	4,393,000	4,452,000	4,599,000	4,639,000
Percent Change	+0.04%	+2.6%	-2.5%	+2.0%	+0.7%	+1.3%	+3.3%	+0.9%
NATO/Pact Ratio	1.53:1	1.48:1	1.42:1	1.31:1	1.22:1	1.17:1	1.12:1	1.09:1

NATO AND WARSAW PACT ACTIVE-DUTY ARMED FORCES, 1960-1982 (continued)

NATO	1976	1977	1978	1979	1980	1981	1982
Belgium	88,300	85,700	87,100	86,800	87,900	89,500	93,500
Canada	77,900	80,000	80,000	80,000	78,646	79,497	82,858
Denmark	34,700	34,700	34,000	34,650	35,050	32,600	31,200
France	512,900	502,100	502,800	509,300	494,730	504,630	492,850
West Germany	495,000	489,000	489,900	495,000	495,000	495,000	495,000
Greece	199,500	200,000	190,100	184,600	181,500	193,500	206,500
Italy	352,000	333,000	362,000	365,000	366,000	366,000	370,000
Luxembourg	625	625	700	660	660	690	690
Netherlands	112,200	109,700	109,700	114,820	114,980	102,800	103,957
Norway	39,000	39,000	39,000	39,000	37,000	37,000	42,100
Portugal	59,800	58,800	63,500	60,500	59,540	70,926	66,426
Turkey	480,000	465,000	485,000	566,000	567,000	569,000	569,000
United Kindgom	344,150	339,200	313,000	322,891	329,204	343,646	327,600
United States	2,086,700	2,088,000	2,068,800	2,022,000	2,050,000	2,049,100	2,116,800
Total	4,882,775	4,824,825	4,825,900	4,881,221	4,897,210	4,933,259	4,998,481
Percent Change	-3.7%	-1.2%	+0.02%	+1.1%	+0.3%	+0.7%	+1.3%
U.S. Share	42.7%	43.3%	42.9%	41.4%	41.9%	41.5%	42.3%

Warsaw Pact	1976	1977	1978	1979	1980	1981	1982
Soviet Union	3,650,000	3,675,000	3,638,000	3,658,000	3,658,000	3,673,000	3,705,000
Rumania	181,000	180,000	180,500	180,500	184,500	184,500	181,000
Poland	290,000	307,000	306,500	317,500	317,500	319,500	317,000
Czechoslovakia	180,000	181,000	186,000	194,000	195,000	194,000	196,500
Bulgaria	164,000	148,500	150,000	150,000	149,000	149,000	148,000
East Germany	157,000	157,000	157,000	159,000	162,000	167,000	166,000
Hungary	100,000	103,000	114,000	104,000	93,000	101,000	106,000
Total	4,722,000	4,751,000	4,732,000	4,763,000	4,759,000	4,788,000	4,819,500
Percent Change	+1.8%	+0.6%	-0.4%	+0.7%	-0.1%	+0.6%	+0.66%
NATO/Pact Ratio	1.03:1	1.015:1	1.02:1	1.025:1	1.029:1	1.03:1	1.037:1

NOTE: The data presented in the Appendix are based on estimates compiled by the Institute for Strategic Studies (London) and published annually in *The Military Balance*.

France is included in the NATO totals because it has continued as a member of the political alliance and French forces cooperate quietly with those of other member governments. Iceland is not included because it maintains no armed forces. Spain is excluded since it did not formally join NATO until 1982.

Albania is excluded from Warsaw Pact totals because it broke diplomatic relations with the Soviet Union in 1960 and thereafter did not participate at all in Warsaw Pact activities.

The estimates for the NATO countries are conservative in that the NATO Information Service credits the NATO countries with higher totals than does the ISS (see *NATO: Facts and Figures*, 10th ed. [Brussels: NATO Information Service, 1981], p. 322).

[a]After mobilization.

NOTES

1. See, for example, "Did You Say Allies?," *The Economist*, 6/6/81; Stanley Hoffmann, "NATO and Nuclear Weapons: Reasons and Unreason," *Foreign Affairs* 60, 2 (Winter 1981/1982); James Goldsborough, "The Roots of Western Disunity," *New York Times Magazine*, 5/9/82; and John Newhouse, "Arms and Allies," *The New Yorker*, 2/28/83.

2. See, for example, Earl Ravenal, *NATO's Unremarked Demise* (Berkeley: Institute of International Studies, 1979); Irving Kristol, "Does NATO Exist?," *Washington Quarterly* 2, 4 (Autumn 1979), and "NATO at a Dead End," *Wall Street Journal*, 7/15/81; and William Pfaff, "Reflections: The Waiting Nations," *The New Yorker*, 1/3/83.

3. On this point, see Gregory Treverton, "Nuclear Weapons in Europe," *Adelphi Papers* 168 (Summer 1981); Uwe Nerlich, "Theater Nuclear Forces in Europe: Is NATO Running Out of Options?," *Washington Quarterly* 3, 1 (Winter 1980); Catherine Kelleher, "The Present as Prologue: Europe and Theater Nuclear Modernization," *International Security* 5, 4 (Spring 1981); Christopher Bertram, "The Implications of Theater Nuclear Weapons in Europe," *Foreign Affairs* 60, 2 (Winter 1981/1982); and Morton Halperin, "NATO and the TNF Controversy: Threats to the Alliance," *Orbis* 26, 1 (Spring 1982).

4. Helmut Schmidt, "The 1977 Alastair Buchan Memorial Lecture," *Survival* 20, 1 (January/February 1978). An excellent account of the concerns that led Schmidt to raise this issue can be found in Raymond Garthoff, "The NATO Decision on Theater Nuclear Forces," *Political Science Quarterly* 98, 2 (Summer 1983): 199-200.

5. Treverton, pp. 22-24; Garthoff, pp. 198-204; Newhouse, p. 64.

6. Kelleher, pp. 152-53; Garthoff, pp. 202-4.

7. See, for example, Joseph Joffe, "European-American Relations: The Enduring Crisis," *Foreign Affairs* 59, 4 (Spring 1981): 838; Goldsborough, p. 49; and John Vinocur, "The German Malaise," *New York Times Magazine*, 11/15/81, pp. 116-17.

8. For the argument that there is a trend toward neutralism and pacifism in Western Europe, see Kristol, "NATO at a Dead End," and William Schneider, "Elite and Public Opinion: The Alliance's New Fissure," *Public Opinion* 6,

1 (February/March 1983). For the "successor generation" argument, see Walter Laqueur, "Euro-neutralism," *Commentary*, June 1980; Vinocur; and Stephen Szabo, "The Successor Generation in Europe," *Public Opinion* 6, 1 (February/March 1983). Both arguments are combined in another essay by Laqueur: "Hollanditis: A New Stage in European Neutralism," *Commentary*, August 1981.

9. Edmond Taylor, "The Atlantic Alliance: After Gruenther, What?," *The Reporter*, 6/2/55, p. 18. See also the discussion of "growing tendencies of anti-NATO feeling in Germany" in Hans Speier, *German Rearmament and Atomic War* (Evanston: Row, Peterson & Co., 1957), p. 218.

10. Elisabeth Noelle-Neumann, "Are the Germans 'Collapsing' or 'Standing Firm'?," *Encounter* 58, 2 (February 1982): 77.

11. Schneider, p. 6.

12. Richard and Anna Merritt, *Public Opinion in Semisovereign Germany* (Urbana: University of Illinois Press, 1980), p. 25.

13. Karl Deutsch, Lewis Edinger, Roy Macridis, Richard Merritt, *France, Germany and the Western Alliance* (New York: Charles Scribner's Sons, 1967), p. 181n. In another 1964 poll, 33 percent of West German respondents indicated a preference for staying out of big power politics and concentrating on domestic welfare, 43 percent rejected that attitude, and 24 percent were uncertain (*ibid.*, p. 180n).

14. Karen DeYoung, "European People Favor Limited Backing for U.S.," *Washington Post*, 4/17/80.

15. Kenneth Adler and Douglas Wertman, "Is NATO in Trouble?: A Survey of European Attitudes," *Public Opinion* 4, 4 (August/September 1981): 10.

16. *Ibid.*, p. 9.

17. Schneider, p. 6. See also Adler and Wertman, p. 10; and Werner Kaltefleiter, "German Divisions," *Policy Review* 18 (August/September 1981).

18. Jan Stapel, "Surveys by Netherlands Gallup Affiliate Reveal Extent of 'Hollanditis'," *The Gallup Report* 208 (January 1983): 21.

19. Adler and Wertman, p. 10.

20. *World Opinion Update* 4, 2 (March/April 1980): 33. See also Adler and Wertman, p. 10; and Elisabeth Noelle-Neumann, "Polls Favor Good Relationship with United States," *Capital*, August 1981 [Foreign Broadcast Information Service (FBIS) translation].

21. Elisabeth Noelle-Neumann, "In West Germany, Conservative Mood Isn't Helping the Conservative Candidate," *Public Opinion* 3, 4 (August/September 1980): 44, and "Polls Favor Good Relationship with United States," p. 32.

22. See, for example, the articles by Laqueur, Goldsborough, Hoffmann, Pfaff, and Szabo cited above.

23. Adler and Wertman, p. 10. See also Kaltefleiter, p. 42.

24. Kaltefleiter, pp. 44-45.

25. *World Opinion Update* 4, 2 (March/April 1980), p. 42.

26. Noelle-Neumann, "Polls Favor Good Relationship with United States," p. 33.

27. See, for example, Laqueur, "Hollanditis: A New Stage in European Neutralism," pp. 19, 24-25; Kristol, "NATO at a Dead End"; William Safire, "Helmut's Pipeline," *New York Times*, 2/19/82, p. 27; Walter Hahn, "Does NATO Have a Future?," *International Security Review* 5, 2 (Summer 1980): 155-56; and Stephen Haseler, "The Euromissile Crisis," *Commentary*, May 1983, p. 31.

28. A good example is Laqueur's use of a leak to the press that Denmark was considering a freeze on military spending that would cause the Danish army to lose one-fourth of its effective strength and the Danish navy one-third of its ships ("Hollanditis: A New Stage in European Neutralism," p. 24). From 1981 to 1982, Danish active-duty forces declined from 32,600 to 31,200; the Danish army lost 1300 personnel; the navy gained 100; and the air force lost 200. These cuts were at least partly the result of a severe recession: Danish GNP declined by 0.9 percent in 1980 and by 1.0 percent in 1981 (Institute for Strategic Studies, *The Military Balance, 1981-1982*, p. 31; *1982-1983*, pp. 33-34).

29. Lord Ismay, *NATO: The First Five Years* (Paris: 1954), pp. 110-12.

30. Samuel Huntington, *The Common Defense* (New York: Columbia University Press, 1961), pp. 79, 95; Coral Bell, *Negotiation from Strength* (London: Chatto and Windus, 1962), p. 138; Institute for Strategic Studies, *The Communist Bloc and the Free World: The Military Balance, 1960*, pp. 13-14; Institute for Strategic Studies, *The Military Balance, 1971-1972*, p. 63.

31. Reconstruction proceeded very slowly; by 1960, total Hungarian active-duty forces numbered only about 75,000. Reliable data on East European armed forces during the 1950s are exceedingly difficult to compile. The figures cited here are from *Statesman's Yearbook, 1951; 1957; 1960-1961; 1961-1962;* and from ISS, *The Military Balance, 1960*, p. 6; *1971-1972*, p. 63.

32. Roger Hilsman, "NATO: The Developing Strategic Context," in *NATO and American Security* ed. Klaus Knorr (Princeton: Princeton University Press, 1959), pp. 23-24, 33. See also Alain Enthoven and K. Wayne Smith, *How Much is Enough?* (New York: Harper & Row, 1971), pp. 140-41.

33. On these points, see the following volumes of Institute for Strategic Studies, *The Military Balance: 1964-1965*, pp. 15-25; *1966-1967*, p. 27; *1968-1969*, pp. 18-32; *1969-1970*, p. 5. See also U.S. Department of Defense, *Annual Report for FY1982*, p. B5.

34. Enthoven and Smith, pp. 147-49, 151, 154-56.

35. Clarence A. Robinson, Jr., "Increasing Soviet Offensive Threat Spurs Stronger Europe Air Arm," *Aviation Week and Space Technology*, 8/1/77, pp. 38, 45-46.

36. Institute for Strategic Studies, *The Military Balance, 1977-1978*, p. 6.

37. On these points, see Adler and Wertman, p. 9; Kaltefleiter, pp. 46-47; and Connie De Boer, "The Polls: Our Commitment to World War III," *Public Opinion Quarterly* 45, 1 (Spring 1981): 128, 130.

38. On these points, see Clarence A. Robinson, Jr., "Strength Sought at Least Cost," *Aviation Week and Space Technology*, 8/8/77, p. 36; "Short-Term Initiatives Readied by NATO," *Aviation Week and Space Technology*, 8/15/77, pp. 54-55; and "That's Better," *The Economist*, 6/3/78, p. 56. See also "NATO to Have 193,000 Anti-tank Missiles by End '78 Vs. 18,000-20,000 Pact Tanks," *Armed Forces Journal*, January 1978, p. 14.

39. See the articles from *Aviation Week* cited in previous note; see also Bernard Weinraub, "Army to Shift More Men and Equipment to Europe," *New York Times*, 10/19/77, p. A5.

40. Drew Middleton, "NATO Extends 3% Rise in Annual Spending to '85," *New York Times*, 5/16/79, p. A9; Eugene Kozicharow, "NATO Members Urge SALT 3 Parleys," *Aviation Week and Space Technology*, 5/21/79, p. 18.

41. "NATO Approves AWACS Buy," *Aviation Week and Space Technology*, 12/11/78, p. 16.

42. For data on increases in defense spending from 1979 to 1980, see Institute for Strategic Studies, *The Military Balance, 1982-1983*, p. 118.

43. Quoted in Eugene Kozicharow, "Stronger Defense Posture Foreseen by Netherlands," *Aviation Week and Space Technology*, 11/17/80, p. 52.

44. Don Cook, "NATO Appears 'On Target' for Defense Budget," *Los Angeles Times*, 11/24/80, pp. 1, 18. See also "NATO Debates 3% Defense Boost," *Aviation Week and Space Technology*, 12/8/80, p. 14.

45. R. W. Apple, Jr., "Voters Shift to Right, Bolstering NATO's Northern Outpost," *New York Times*, 9/20/81, Sec. 4, p. 5; "A Socialist for Rearmament," *The Economist*, 10/17/81, p. 48.

46. Eugene Kozicharow, "NATO Approaching 3% Growth in 1982," *Aviation Week and Space Technology*, 12/21/81, pp. 57-58.

47. See, for example, Laqueur, "Hollanditis: A New Stage in European Neutralism"; and Haseler.

48. *World Opinion Update* 6, 4 (July/August 1982): 99.

49. February/March 1980 survey, reported in Adler and Wertman, p. 10.

50. De Boer, p. 128; Adler and Wertman, pp. 10-11; Noelle-Neumann, "Are the Germans 'Collapsing' or 'Standing Firm'?," p. 79.

51. Speier, p. 253. See also Merritt and Merritt, p. 240. Speier reports that when those in the September 1955 survey who had opposed American use of nuclear weapons were asked if they would change their views if the Soviets attacked Germany first with nuclear weapons, only 48 out of each 65 who opposed American nuclear retaliation changed their views to be in favor of it.

52. Judith Miller, "Poll Shows Nuclear Freeze Backed If Soviet Doesn't Gain," *New York Times*, 5/30/82, p. 18.

53. De Boer, p. 129; Stapel, p. 21; Noelle-Neumann, "Are the Germans 'Collapsing' or 'Standing Firm'?," p. 78.

54. September 1981 survey, reported in Stapel, pp. 20-21.

55. In a fall 1980 survey, Dutch respondents by a 53 to 39 margin rejected the presence of nuclear weapons on Dutch soil. In an April 1981 survey, 23 percent of British respondents felt that Britain should "abandon nuclear weapons altogether, no matter what other countries do," the same result that occurred in a January 1983 survey. See Adler and Wertman, p. 50; *World Opinion Update* 7, 2 (February 1983): 20.

56. Norbert Muhlen, "The Young Germans and the New Army," *The Reporter*, 1/13/55, p. 25. See also Gordon Craig, "NATO and the New German Army," in *Military Policy and National Security* ed. William Kaufmann (Princeton: Princeton University Press, 1956), p. 200.

57. Lewis Edinger, *West German Rearmament* (Documentary Research Division, Research Studies Institute, Air University, 1955), p. 136. See also Craig, p. 220.

58. Edinger, p. 135. See also Merritt and Merritt, p. 20.

59. Muhlen, p. 26. A November 1954 poll also showed 50 percent of all West German respondents opposed to the creation of an independent German military force, and 79 percent opposed to military service for the youth of Germany (Edinger, p. 137).

60. Muhlen, p. 24; Craig, p. 199.

61. Craig, p. 219. See also Speier, pp. 153-69.

62. On this, see Edinger, pp. 95-98; see also Speier, pp. 167-69.

63. See Craig, pp. 225-26. See also Gordon Craig, "Germany and NATO: The Rearmament Debate, 1950-1958," in Knorr, ed., pp. 240-41.

64. Craig, "NATO and the New German Army," p. 256, and "Germany and NATO: The Rearmament Debate, 1950-1958," p. 241. See also Speier, p. 182.

65. Craig, "NATO and the New German Army," p. 227. See also Speier, pp. 183-86.

66. Craig, "Germany and NATO: The Rearmament Debate, 1950-1958," p. 242. See also Speier, pp. 187-88, 207-10.

67. On Adenauer's shift, see Craig, "Germany and NATO: The Rearmament Debate, 1950-1958." pp. 242-43; and Speier, pp. 211-12, 219.

68. Craig, "Germany and NATO: The Rearmament Debate, 1950-1958," p. 244. See also Speier, p. 220.

69. On the Kampf dem Atomtod, see Craig, "Germany and NATO: The Rearmament Debate, 1950-1958," pp. 246-48. See also Jeffrey Boutwell, "Politics and the Peace Movement in West Germany," *International Security* 7, 4 (Spring 1983): 74-75.

70. Hoffmann, p. 328.

71. Karl Deutsch and Lewis Edinger, *Germany Rejoins the Powers* (Stanford: Stanford University Press, 1958), p. 27. See also Boutwell, p. 76.

72. Adler and Wertman, p. 50. See also Noelle-Neumann "Are the Germans 'Collapsing' or 'Standing Firm'?," p. 81.

73. Klaas de Vries, "Responding to the SS-20: An Alternative Approach," *Survival* 21, 6 (November/December 1979), p. 254.

74. U.S. Department of State, *Foreign Relations of the United States*, 1948, v. 2, p. 281.

75. Adler and Wertman, p. 9 (emphasis in original). See also Kaltefleiter, p. 46; De Boer, p. 129; and *World Opinion Update* 6, 3 (May/June 1982): 71.

76. Commission of the European Communities, *Euro-barometre* 16 (December 1981): 9.

77. Schneider, pp. 5-6; Haseler, p. 28.

78. Werner Kaltefleiter, "Germans: Friendlier but Apprehensive," *Public Opinion* 2, 2 (March/May 1979): 11.

79. Lawrence Freedman, "Limited War; Unlimited Protest," *Orbis* 26, 1 (Spring 1982): 99.

80. See Robert Osgood, *NATO: The Entangling Alliance* (Chicago: University of Chicago Press, 1962).

81. McGeorge Bundy, "America in the 1980s: Reframing Our Relations with Our Friends and Among Our Allies," *Survival* 24, 1 (January/February 1982): 27.

82. Bertram, pp. 324-25.

83. Francois de Rose, "Updating Deterrence in Europe: Inflexible Response?," *Survival* 24, 1 (January/February 1982), p. 22.

84. Quoted in Drew Middleton, "NATO Chief Glum on Allies' Resolve," *New York Times*, 9/18/81, p. 3.

85. Robert Kennedy, "Soviet Theater-Nuclear Forces: Implications for NATO Defense," *Orbis* 25, 2 (Summer 1981): 341-42.

86. Bundy, p. 27.

87. Treverton, pp. 12-17.

WALLACE J. THIES is Assistant Professor of Political Science at the University of California, Berkeley. During 1979 and 1980, he worked in the U.S. State Department's Bureau of Politico-Military Affairs as an International Affairs Fellow of the Council on Foreign Relations. He is author of *When Governments Collide: Coercion and Diplomacy in the Vietnam Conflict, 1964-1968* (Berkeley: University of California Press, 1980).

INSTITUTE OF INTERNATIONAL STUDIES
UNIVERSITY OF CALIFORNIA, BERKELEY

215 Moses Hall   Berkeley, California 94720

CARL G. ROSBERG, *Director*

Monographs published by the Institute include:

RESEARCH SERIES

1. *The Chinese Anarchist Movement.* R.A. Scalapino and G.T. Yu. ($1.00)
7. *Birth Rates in Latin America.* O. Andrew Collver. ($2.50)
15. *Central American Economic Integration.* Stuart I. Fagan. ($2.00)
16. *The International Imperatives of Technology.* Eugene B. Skolnikoff. ($2.95)
17. *Autonomy or Dependence in Regional Integration.* P.C. Schmitter. ($1.75)
19. *Entry of New Competitors in Yugoslav Market Socialism.* S.R. Sacks. ($2.50)
20. *Political Integration in French-Speaking Africa.* Abdul A. Jalloh. ($3.50)
21. *The Desert & the Sown: Nomads in Wider Society.* Ed. C. Nelson. ($5.50)
22. *U.S.-Japanese Competition in International Markets.* J.E. Roemer. ($3.95)
23. *Political Disaffection Among British University Students.* J. Citrin and D.J. Elkins. ($2.00)
24. *Urban Inequality and Housing Policy in Tanzania.* Richard E. Stren. ($2.95)
25. *The Obsolescence of Regional Integration Theory.* Ernst B. Haas. ($4.95)
26. *The Voluntary Service Agency in Israel.* Ralph M. Kramer. ($2.00)
27. *The SOCSIM Microsimulation Program.* E. A. Hammel et al. ($4.50)
28. *Authoritarian Politics in Communist Europe.* Ed. Andrew C. Janos. ($3.95)
29. *The Anglo-Icelandic Cod War of 1972-1973.* Jeffrey A. Hart. ($2.00)
30. *Plural Societies and New States.* Robert Jackson. ($2.00)
31. *Politics of Oil Pricing in the Middle East, 1970-75.* R.C. Weisberg. ($4.95)
32. *Agricultural Policy and Performance in Zambia.* Doris J. Dodge. ($4.95)
33. *Five Classy Computer Programs.* E.A. Hammel & R.Z. Deuel. ($3.75)
34. *Housing the Urban Poor in Africa.* Richard E. Stren. ($5.95)
35. *The Russian New Right: Right-Wing Ideologies in USSR.* A. Yanov. ($5.95)
36. *Social Change in Romania, 1860-1940.* Ed. Kenneth Jowitt. ($4.50)
37. *The Leninist Response to National Dependency.* Kenneth Jowitt. ($4.95)
38. *Socialism in Sub-Saharan Africa.* Eds. C. Rosberg & T. Callaghy. ($12.95)
39. *Tanzania's Ujamaa Villages: Rural Development Strategy.* D. McHenry. ($5.95)
40. *Who Gains from Deep Ocean Mining?* I.G. Bulkley. ($3.50)
41. *Industrialization & the Nation-State in Peru.* Frits Wils. ($5.95)
42. *Ideology, Public Opinion, & Welfare Policy: Taxes and Spending in Indus-dustrialized Societies.* R.M. Coughlin. ($6.50)
43. *The Apartheid Regime: Political Power and Racial Domination.* Eds. R.M. Price and C. G. Rosberg. ($12.50)
44. *Yugoslav Economic System in the 1970s.* L.D. Tyson. ($5.50)
45. *Conflict in Chad.* Virginia Thompson & Richard Adloff. ($7.50)
46. *Conflict and Coexistence in Belgium.* Ed. Arend Lijphart. ($7.50)

47. *Changing Realities in Southern Africa.* Ed. Michael Clough. ($12.50)
48. *Nigerian Women Mobilized: Women's Political Activity in Southern Nigeria,
    1900-1965.* Nina Emma Mba. ($12.95)
49. *Institutions of Rural Development for the Poor.* Ed. D. Leonard & D.
    Marshall. ($11.50)
50. *Politics of Women & Work in USSR & U.S.* J.C. Moses. ($9.50)
51. *Zionism and Territory.* Baruch Kimmerling. ($12.50)
52. *Soviet Subsidization of Trade with Eastern Europe.* M. Marrese & J. Vanous.
    ($14.50)
53. *Voluntary Efforts in Decentralized Management.* L. Ralston et al. ($9.00)

POLITICS OF MODERNIZATION SERIES

1. *Spanish Bureaucratic-Patrimonialism in America.* M. Sarfatti. ($2.00)
2. *Civil-Military Relations in Argentina, Chile, & Peru.* L. North. ($2.00)
9. *Modernization & Bureaucratic-Authoritarianism: Studies in South American
   Politics.* Guillermo O'Donnell. ($8.95)

POLICY PAPERS IN INTERNATIONAL AFFAIRS

1. *Images of Detente & the Soviet Political Order.* K. Jowitt. ($1.25)
2. *Detente After Brezhnev: Domestic Roots of Soviet Policy.* A. Yanov. ($4.50)
3. *Mature Neighbor Policy: A New Policy for Latin America.* A. Fishlow. ($3.95)
4. *Five Images of Soviet Future: Review & Synthesis.* G.W. Breslauer. ($4.50)
5. *Global Evangelism Rides Again: How to Protect Human Rights Without
   Really Trying.* E.B. Haas. ($2.95)
6. *Israel & Jordan: An Adversarial Partnership.* Ian Lustick. ($2.00)
7. *Political Syncretism in Italy.* Giuseppe Di Palma. ($3.95)
8. *U.S. Foreign Policy in Sub-Saharan Africa.* R.M. Price. ($4.50)
9. *East-West Technology Transfer in Perspective.* R.J. Carrick. ($5.50)
10. *NATO's Unremarked Demise.* Earl C. Ravenal. ($3.50)
11. *Toward Africanized Policy for Southern Africa.* R. Libby. ($5.50)
12. *Taiwan Relations Act & Defense of ROC.* E. Snyder et al. ($7.50)
13. *Cuba's Policy in Africa, 1959-1980.* William M. LeoGrande. ($4.50)
14. *Norway, NATO, & Forgotten Soviet Challenge.* K. Amundsen. ($2.95)
15. *Japanese Industrial Policy.* Ira Magaziner and Thomas Hout. ($6.50)
16. *Containment, Soviet Behavior, & Grand Strategy.* Robert Osgood. ($5.50)
17. *U.S.-Japanese Competition in Semiconductor Industry.* M. Borrus et al.
    ($7.50)